LEADERSHIP: THE HUMAN RACE

LEADERSHIP
✦
The Human Race

GUY D. CHARLTON

1992
JUTA & CO, LTD

First published in 1992

Copyright © Juta & Co, Ltd
PO Box 14373, Kenwyn 7790

ISBN 0 7021 2800 7

Printed and bound in South Africa by
The Rustica Press, Ndabeni, Cape.

D1503

FOREWORD

It is essential, in building South African organisations and institutions, that we develop appropriate leadership and management technologies. The uniqueness of the South African conditions in terms of diversity and dynamic complexity require that we look beyond the quick fix or the latest trend. We need to look into the philosophy and values that will underpin future organisations capable of sustainable competitive advantage.

Leadership development is one of the high-leverage areas to achieve this advantage. Guy Charlton's book takes a major step towards achieving this. While he has utilised world-class thinking and international practice, he has grounded it in South African research to provide a practical competency base from which to develop local leadership. He emphasises learning as a basis on which organisations can build to achieve extraordinary results — an approach rapidly gaining support in the West.

I have found that two aspects of organisational culture provide useful indicators of organisational ability to learn: fear and arrogance. When either of these are present, organisations have severe difficulty in learning.

Our philosophy and values provide a basis for the knowledge of how to make organisations function effectively, and for the skills required to lead and manage such organisations.

v

In respect of our values underpinning leadership and day-to-day operational practices, this contribution by Guy Charlton is a bold step in the right direction.

LOUIS VAN DER MERWE
Innovation Associates of South Africa (Pty) Ltd

PREFACE

The whirlwind gathered momentum fuelled by the winds of exponential change. Round and round hurtles a world out of control — uprooting hope borne out of a lack of vision, greed, timidity and authoritarian decree. Chaos sweeps away the guiding anchors and carefully drafted plans of every nation and organisation into the black centre — but the centre cannot hold.

The old order of reactive quick fixes, immediate gratification and 'bigger is better' would no longer suffice. The pleasure principle and the power principle had been built on quicksand. Instead, the permanent, pervasive cry of the human heart rose up from every family; from the small business and multi-national corporation; from every poverty stricken nation to the tie-pinned brokers on Wall Street. The cry for a better world — for a sense of meaning and a guiding beacon of hope was indicative of the despair at every level of national and international life. It was indicative of the pervasive incapacity of alienated leaders to put the humanity back into organisations; to find the human touch.

The need for leadership has never been so great. The stage for Armageddon and the consequent seeking for people of character has never been better set. Indeed the axiom behind successful human endeavour, be it a family, business, political, sporting, spiritual or national level, can be summed up in one word — Leadership.

The impact of the decisions and indecisions of leaders underpin the conversation in every boardroom and family meal. Will I be safe tonight? Will I have a job tomorrow and will my company survive in an ever changing environment? What will the future political changes mean for me? Who, if anyone, can I trust — especially if my boss is hedging his bets — and the question becomes how to get money out of the country and get a second passport? How will we cope with the increase in busfare, housing and company tax? — How will we fuel economic growth and redistribute wealth? Is there a future for our children; and, perhaps most pertinent of all — will the hard work and preparation for my future make any difference in the long run?

On the lighter side, the performance of our favourite sporting teams are dependent on their leadership. Even on an individual level, the lone runner's performance is dependent on his/her ability to manage and lead him/herself in the pursuit of excellence. The child's mother takes on a key leadership and developmental role to her children as does the lioness and the queen ant in the animal kingdom.

In short, our quality of life is dependent on the quality of our leaders. The greatest single investment **you** can make in your own future, and the future of the country, is to learn to be a competent leader both professionally and privately.

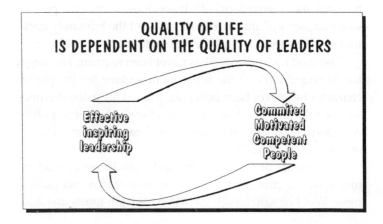

ASPIRATIONS vs EXPECTATIONS

Effective leadership is not about position power in the organisational hierarchy but about personal power that enables us to create our own future as well as our own quality of life. It is about being responsible to yourself and to others. It is about serving and stewardship which engenders commitment, rather than egocentric behaviour that can at best offer compliance.

Leadership is about creating realistic expectations (what you owe me) and balancing these with aspirations (what I/we can strive to create) — and then creating a context where aspirations can be realised. Leadership that does the right thing at the right time and enables ordinary people to accomplish extraordinary things can no longer be the preserve of the 'man at the top'. The challenge of leadership faces every person in every role in every society. An organisation's ability to survive is directly dependent on growing leaders and this in turn is dependent on meeting the cry of the human heart — of putting humanity back into organisations. An organisation's ability, skill and commitment to enable, empower and liberate human resources will be it's only source of competitive advantage in the future. In this respect, it is a race — The Human Race.

TABLE OF CONTENTS

INTRODUCTION

'Managerial work is undergoing such enormous and rapid changes that managers are inventing their profession as they go. In short, leadership is more difficult, yet more critical than ever'[1]

This book aims to bridge the gap between leadership demand and supply (and between theory and practice). It deals with the why, what, and most importantly, the how of leadership development. Too often well meaning managers attend seminars elaborating on the multitude of problems facing them, without receiving any practical guidelines on how to constructively cope with these on the job. All this does is perpetuate a sense of hopelessness and apathy, as well as encouraging the ostrich syndrome of burying one's head in the sand. The world does not need prophets of doom expounding the pathway of destruction, but rather people of action who offer a realistic vision of an attractive future and a plan of how to get there — together.

The text is based on the actual strategies of excellent leaders and how specific competencies can be developed and accelerated within organisations. In this respect, it is *how* the leadership difference, can make the difference to the quality and productivity of individual and organisational life.

My journey into leadership started some ten years ago with a desire to understand individual growth and change. This led me to work in Soweto and Alexandra townships and a 'grassroots' year in the bush prompting the realisation that an exclusive focus on the individual was somewhat idealistic and insufficient to bring about meaningful organisational change which significantly *contributed* to individual discomfort. Simultaneously, my focus also changed from intensive work with individual 'pathological patients' (at TARA hospital in Johannesburg) toward unhealthy environments which encouraged mediocrity and generated the enormous stress of everyday living.

Ultimately I entered into the world of business with two fundamental realisations :

❏ 'He who pays the piper calls the tune'
❏ Business offers a fundamental leverage for change, a 'locus of innovation' where new ideas get put into practice and fuel economic and societal development.

The questions I was asking also moved from a focus on the reasons for suffering to a focus on factors underpinning excellence. What made the difference between an average and an excellent individual or organisation? What kind of environment encouraged outstanding performance that significantly impacted on a company's bottom line? Was there an alternative beneficial both to the company and the individual to the power struggles and depersonalised numbers game? In other words, could the piper play a different tune when the needs of the organisation and of the individual were in step? Rather than propagating a philosophical jive, the only alternative was to find out what tune successful organisations were playing and how they had learnt to dance. Once these critical factors had been identified, the challenge became that of *implementing* them through strategic training and development in a fraction of the time that it had taken organisations to learn the lessons of success.

This book is an account of this journey and is based on extensive research concerning what constitutes leadership competence, both nationally and internationally. The good news is that leadership is not some mystical quality that the privileged few have inherited. Indeed, leaders testify to hard work and trial and error through pragmatic learning.[2] In other words, leadership is both an art and a discipline that *can* be learnt, if people are willing to pay the price for change.

It is interesting to note that many of the critical competencies of leadership are similar wholewide, and common across political, business, sporting, social, spiritual and educational contexts. The key ingredients to any leadership activity are attitudes and behaviour that empower people to go the extra mile and to create an environment where people are willing, able and allowed to perform to their potential.

As previously mentioned, leadership is a skill that anyone in a position of responsibility needs to cultivate. In fact, the competencies described in this book, although aimed primarily at the upper echelons of South African business, are equally trainable to the average worker. I have just spent the last eighteen months developing leaders as part of a massive equal opportunity programme in the Chamber of Mines, with most of the group comprising black men and women with a standard eight education. Simultaneously, I have been working top down in developing leadership competence in order to accelerate the promotion of people into managerial positions. While the method, process, structure and application of the two groups differ, the competencies required to perform successfully at work are the same : The need to capture people's attention through a vision (or goal) to work towards; the ability to communicate this in a meaningful (motivational) way; the need to develop trust; and the ability to manage yourself before you try to manage others, thus resulting in the empowerment of people who *choose* to be productive, efficient, and cost effective.

There is, however, bad news too. The development of leadership competence is no quick fix. The vast majority of formal and informal management development activities worldwide have failed. Research has constantly highlighted the fact that business schools and universities have failed to teach relevant managerial and leadership skills. Instead business leaders attribute very little of their success to 'formal education'.[3] The training and development profession has an equally dismal record.[4] Trainers have tended to focus on the 'flavour of the month' packaged courses, said to cure every corporate ill, without understanding the complexities of individual and organisational change.

There has also been a question mark over the transference of knowledge to the workplace which significantly impacts on a department's productivity. This is why the notion of competence is vital to leadership development. Competence is defined as the exhibition of specific behaviour and attitudes being clearly demonstrated and therefore measurable, and is vastly different to inherent potential to perform. Any manager, when he spends money on training wants a return on investment. He/she wants to know the specific capabilities of people when they return in order to make the department perform better.

There is another problem that inhibits the success of leadership development. Most learning takes place on the job, because the reward and sanction for behaviour rests with the immediate boss. Consequently, if the organisation does not encourage a learning environment and managers do not take their fundamental responsibilities to empower people seriously, then any development is fruitless. People will simply be empowered to leave the organisation and be drawn to those that do foster personal growth.

Training is only one part of a strategic effort to get the right people in the right place at the right time. Human resource development is dependent on the alignment and complimentarity of the business plan, selection criteria, evaluation, reward system and organisational development/culture efforts. Unless training is part of the total organisational change process, then it becomes no more than a 'band-aid' covering deeper problems.

Finally, most attempts at leadership development fail because the process requires a fundamental shift of heart and mind. Getting the best out of people presupposes a view that they are indeed creative and competent. In contrast, most organisations are built on structured hierarchies and political power struggles — which are founded on the premise of peoples incompetence, and consequently evoke a self-fulfilling prophecy. Although most leaders deny this control orientation, a deeper look at the way human beings are managed reveals structures that inhibit creativity and responsibility. In this respect apartheid (us and them) is still alive and well in many businesses. A change of mind is also essential for the leader who forgoes the security of a simplistic cause-effect thought process to embrace the interrelationships and patterns underlying events, consequently intervening in a way that has maximum impact. Essentially, this change starts with *you* and the development of yourself as an instrument of change, which is fundamental in creating a better future.

Most training and education efforts ignore the deeper issues of attitudinal, even spiritual change that is fundamental to leadership. No amount of skills training will be effective if the underlying attitude of the person is contrary to the development of the human spirit within the organisation. Leadership then is a transformational experience, where first the individual is transformed and then in turn transforms/converts followers into leaders and agents of change. This can only happen if leaders are willing to acknowledge the diversity and uniqueness of people and abandon themselves to serving them while giving up the payoffs of control that destroy the human spirit.

This book attempts to provide practical guidelines to overcome these problems of training in general and specifically, the development of leadership competence. Although examples are primarily drawn from South African business leaders — as this has been the context of my research and experience — the book is relevant to any person who is concerned with creating a context where people are the key to achieving extraordinary results. This could take the form of coaching a rowing crew, a teacher in a classroom, religious organisations, empowering constituents in a political organisation or optimising productivity and relationships in a business context, even the home executive faced with the challenge of nuturing and leading her children.

While a model of leadership development will be proposed as a strategic guideline for implementation, this book is simply intended as a catalyst toward significant training (that makes a difference) — and not the alpha and omega of leadership. Let us debate the issues, learn, and share experiences that work. Your future and the future of your organisation is dependent upon it.

ORIENTATION

The chapters in the book are generally sequential and build on each other. Chapter I explores the fundamental importance of leadership — particularly in business but also in other spheres of human endeavour. Chapter II looks briefly at the changing human context of leadership and the necessity of entering the human race. Chapters III and IV define what leadership is not (difference between leadership and management) and specific leadership competencies that comprise South African business leadership.

Interestingly, the South African research complimented international research — which suggested that leaders regardless of context apply the core competencies of vision, meaning/communication, trust and the management of self. However, South African leaders also empowered their followers — suggesting that empowerment is both a consequence and specific competence of leadership. This points to the fundamental role leaders have in developing people and impacting on the country's skills shortage.

While there is increasing clarity concerning the broad competencies of leadership, confusion will exist as to the specific measurable behaviours that comprise the above five competencies.

Chapters V–IX discuss specific leadership competencies, drawing on examples of South African leaders. Together, these twenty-five competencies can be used as a basis to identify effective leadership within South African organisations.

Although these chapters all compliment one another, they are also intended to add value to existing literature on each specific competence.

Chapter X offers an explanation for the difference between effective and ineffective leadership as an introduction to the last chapter concerning strategic leadership development.

The entire book is written with a view to offering constructive guidelines for the development of leadership within organisations. This of necessity, demands a multifaceted approach involving a fundamental shift of attitude—in order to survive and thrive in the Human Race.

CHAPTER I

WHY LEADERSHIP?

INTRODUCTION

Mission statements and chairman's reports abound with the concept of excellence. Every year the corporate strategists, with the diligence of artists creating a new landscape, flock together to draft a plan for success and survival. Regular as clockwork, the lofty concepts of quality, service and customer focus are extolled. More recently, the necessity of being an 'equal opportunity employer' has surfaced, together with the vague notion of 'being the best' or being leaders in our field and producing 'state of the art' products. Then, of course, the concept of our human resources as our greatest asset and what the company is doing in this regard is included — all with the best intentions.

However, one of the most difficult challenges of any person in a leadership position is the ability to translate intention into action and then to sustain it. There are a multitude of restraining factors that erode the best laid strategic plans. Broadly (and briefly) speaking, what are the factors in the external environment that inhibit the realisation of excellence?

❏ Uncertainty and anxiety pervade the socio-political and business environment — which tends to push decision-makers into a reactive, 'wait and see' stability orientation toward risk and change

❏ Exponential change and increasing world class competition

1

❏ A commitment, credibility and productivity crisis
❏ Escalating shortage of executive and technical skills
❏ South African managers that are among the most stressed in the world[1] and a third world population that is (at least) as stressed — albeit for different reasons

Given these and other problems, how does any organisation obtain excellence?

Most of the time the answers I am giving deal with training, training and more training. The question then arises — training for what, and how can training make people more productive and better able to cope with the above challenges?

The first hurdle to overcome is that of a *commitment* to training and a belief that the process can in fact make a difference. Japan spends approximately fifteen times more on training as South African companies. Many South African companies pay lip service to the notion of investing in human resources. This could be in part due to not knowing *how to invest in human resource development*, which in turn could be a reflection of the competence of the human resource department.

C.E.O. — CRITICAL SUCCESS FACTORS

The question of *what* to train, is best answered by asking recognised leaders what they perceive to be critical success factors in business. Research by Gail Kelly involving twenty five successful business leaders highlights the following factors considered to be fundmental to success.

❏ Leadership
❏ Motivating people and interpersonal issues
❏ Ability to learn on the job
❏ Linking strategic planning to implementation
❏ Hard work[2]

IS MANAGEMENT DEVELOPMENT A HOAX?

The obvious question arises as to whether these critical success skills are being trained effectively.

International research has constantly highlighted the fact that managers and chief executive officers perceive formal management training as having contributed very little toward their overall success.[3] Business schools have been criticised for 'miseducation' with their focus on methods of quantitative analyses and linear thinking rather than 'process' or people competencies such as creativity, intuition and motivation.[4]

An extensive industry wide study found that between 75–90 % of the successful manager's time was spent on interpersonal activities. Managers preferred an active, 'hands on' orientation reacting to the initiatives and needs of others whilst motivating people in a relatively unstructured way.[5] This picture is vastly different from the assumptions underlying many training programmes that teach managers to rationally plan, organise, lead and control.

The climate of uncertainty and ambiguity impacting on business, demands new and innovative paradigms of looking at the world. The outdated notion of rational management needs to be replaced by an understanding of the complex interrelationships and patterns underlying changing conditions and an understanding of individual and organisational growth and change. In short, an understanding of leadership.

GENERATIVE LEARNING — A CHANGE OF HEAD AND HEART

Peter Senge distinguishes between adaptive and generative learning which illustrates the importance of seeing interrelationships rather than thinking in a linear, cause-effect manner. Adaptive learning involves a reactive orientation to changing events, rather than their underlying causes, and consequently is at best a short-term solution.[6] For example, business realises that an alternative to nationalisation and the burgeoning skills shortage is the upward mobility of black people into meaningful managerial positions. Consequently, a massive equal opportunity training programme is embarked upon, focusing on the development of trainees. The thinking goes — 'the cause is insufficient trained managers, therefore, the solution must be training'.

Yet, despite the importance of developing black managers, there has been disturbingly limited progress in the implementation of equal opportunity, with only 9 % of women and 5.5 % of blacks occupying managerial positions.[7] Many companies have found out the hard way that the essential success criteria underpinning equal opportunity includes the visible support of top management, the need to evaluate line managers or their contribution to equity and the focus on introducing complimentary 'white advancement' attitudes prior to any formal training.

The key to any developmental programme is the support and attitude of the line manager who has the power to crush or empower trainees. However, the problem is that as many as 80 % of managers see people as incompetent and therefore evoke a self-fulfilling prophecy of responding to this incompetence.[8] Consequently, any programme that does not simultaneously address these attitudes is simply empowering people to leave the organisation.

Generative thinking focuses on the fundamental causes of problems by viewing life from a systems or interrelationship rather than an event perspective — and consequently offers a crucial leverage point for permanent growth and change.

Any training process that does not take into account the critical determinants of second order or attitudinal change, cannot hope to have a significant impact on organisational effectiveness. Skills-based programmes do have their place in creating first order or behavioural change — but they are unlikely to result in a long-term increase in productivity. Organisational change will only occur with a massive pinpointed effort on these critical leverage points and an alignment of culture, selection, appraisal and reward systems with development efforts.

Leadership offers a fundamental leverage point for organisational change, generative thinking and organisational growth and renewal.

THE RUDDERLESS PLANET

From a business perspective we have seen that excellent managers regard leadership and people issues as fundamental to their success. We have also discovered that formal academic training and informal management development have failed to develop these competencies on the job. This raises the important question as to how, if at all, the gap between the leadership demand-and-supply shortage can be bridged.

The leadership epidemic, far from being limited to business, is a global disease. On an international scale, Warren Bennis points out the three basic dangers to the survival of the human race:

❏ The possibility of a global war
❏ A worldwide epidemic or depression (including famine, collapsed economics and AIDS)
❏ The quality of the leadership of our organisations. Our quality of life is dependent on the qualities of our leaders.[9]

Leadership is the fundamental difference between average and excellent organisations the world over.[10] Consequently, most of the world's problems, expressed through a lack of vision, greed, timidity and authoritarian control, are symptomatic of a leadership crisis at every level of national and international life. Bennis asks the question: 'where have all the leaders gone?' They are, he says, like the words of the haunting folksong 'long time passing'.

PRODUCTIVITY PROBLEMS OR LEADERSHIP CRISIS

There are few South African organisations that do not bemoan the low productivity levels that shackle their growth. Managers complain constantly about the declining work ethic and the 'you owe me a living' mentality of their workforce. Morale in South African companies is at an all time low as the country faces the longest recession in living memory. Uncertainty about job security is the only certainty as retrenchments, like violence, have become a way of life. A recent survey by Fortune Magazine indicates an interesting trend — morale is rapidly declining amongst the American workforce, while many executives appear blissfully unaware of the problem, thinking that it is 'business as usual'.[11]

Herein lies the root of the leadership crisis. The 'average' business leader in my recent research[12], is out of touch with his people. A host of psychological defences are employed in a thinking repertoire that says 'I'm OK, you're not OK. If there is a productivity, commitment or credibility crisis, it is your problem and I have nothing to do with it.' Consequently the need to change them, not me, becomes the power strategy.

The problem with this type of thinking is that it renders the manager powerless, because the solution to the problem lies outside of him/herself. Sure, enormous energy can be used waving the 'big stick' and dangling the 'reward carrot', but these are at best short-term solutions. The manager feels like a victim because motivation is dependent on the whims of the worker.

However, there is another side to the story. Kouzes and Posner point out that leaders can, by definition, only lead if they have followers. They conducted extensive research which showed four essential characteristics that followers expect from leaders: honesty, competence, forward looking and inspiration. Managers who had high credibility and exhibited the above had employees who responded with high commitment to the organisation. Alternatively, managers with low credibility were insensitive and out of touch with their people. This inability to empathise was manifest through arrogance, pride, failure to listen and taking people for granted.[13]

In essence, a commitment and productivity crisis needs to be understood in the context of leaders who have failed to instil vision, a sense of meaning and trust in their followers. A productivity problem tells us as much about the leader as it does the worker. Leaders need to personalise responsibility for creating a context where routine jobs become meaningful; where the human spirit is liberated and people are transformed from a position of working to live, to living to work.

The overwhelming majority of the non-managerial workforce in a recent study said that they could be significantly more effective than they presently are, indicating peoples' intrinsic desire to feel good about their accomplishments at work.[14]

Kouzes and Posner confirm the human desire to be productive:

'Most of us are looking for a calling, not a job. Most of us, like the assembly line worker, have jobs that are too small for our spirits — jobs that are not big enough for people.'[15]

When leaders start to personalise responsibility for creating a productive environment, they put themselves in control of change by committing themselves to learn about leadership competencies. Only by earning commitment can leaders move follower's perceptions from expectations (what the company owes me) to aspirations (what I can contribute to the company).

Granted, there will always be people who come along for a free ride and must be accountable and take the consequences for not performing. Leaders, however, must also take responsibility for giving followers the choice to improve productivity — realising that commitment, motivation and competence is related to effective inspiring leadership.

THE HUMAN RACE

South Africa faces a stark choice if it wants to survive politically and economically. The key to the 'high road' of economic growth and democracy lies in the way we develop and manage our human resources.[16]

This country faces ever declining natural resources, where mining and agriculture account for less than twenty percent of our gross national product. In the future, South Africa's growth will be reliant on the marriage between applied technology and the quality of human competence.

Arie de Geus points out that the need to develop human resources is a world-wide phenomenon. He quotes studies undertaken by the United Nations where the two essential criteria behind successful nations are:

1. The development and management of a country's human resources.

2. Allowing international competition in order to raise the standards and quality of local products and the utilisation of human resources in this regard.[17]

Consequently, the problems or challenges to South Africa are the same as the rest of the world, only different in time, intensity and space.

An exponentially changing environment with increased competitiveness demands the ability to generate new ideas and to react more quickly than competitors. The rate at which a company learns will be its only source of competitive advantage in the future.[18] In the future, economic power will accrue to the company who applies intelligence to the front line.

LEADERSHIP — AN ECONOMIC NECESSITY

'Human capital, defined as the skill, dexterity and knowledge of the population has become the critical input that determines the rate of growth of the economy and the well being of the population .'[19]

It is the competence of managers and, in particular, leaders of people that determines, in large part, the returns that organisations realise from their human capital, or human resources.

The domain of leaders is in creating the future. The unique legacy of the leader is the creation of new institutions that survive over time, through constant organisational growth and renewal. Survival is dependent on the quality of an organisation's leaders and their ability to optimise human resources. This necessitates the empowering of people as a primary competitive strategy.

Empowered employees create systems of their own and consequently, corporate growth and renewal are no longer leader-dependent. With the changing requirements of the information age came the recognition that the 'controller' does not have all the answers. The control orientation, so much a part of the culture of hierarchical organisations, has produced conditioned responders — people who 'hear and receive' only the input for which they have a response. These 'dinosaurs' of the information age are increasingly isolated as they teeter precariously towards the edge of extinction. They have no place in a new world where the creation of new and better products and services at every level of the organisation is a necessity in an increasingly competitive environment.

IT SEEMED LIKE A GOOD IDEA AT THE TIME!

'The long term health of any organisation depends on the quality of people who assume its leadership. Yet, the process by which people are developed and selected for the more senior roles is relatively unplanned and undescribed .'[20]

Given the imperative of the optimisation of a country's human resources, and for creating an environment where this can be realised, the role of leadership within organisations takes on a new meaning. Peter Drucker elaborates on this role:

'The manager is the dynamic, life giving element in every business. Without his/her leadership the resources of production remain resources and never become production. In a competitive economy, above all, the quality and performance of the managers determine the success of a business, indeed they determine its survival. For the quality and performance of its managers is the only competitive advantage an enterprise in a competitive economy can have.'[21]

Yet, despite the importance of developing an organisation's human resources, most companies pay *lip service* to the concept, or alternatively employ naive 'one minute training treatments' that fail to develop essential leadership competencies. Robert Carkhuff elaborates on the problem of ignoring the strategic development of people in organisations:

'Human capital is the source of the next market sensitive idea, while information capital is the operational system for the last idea. While human and information capital will create the future, sources of variance for high performance are either entirely absent or receive token attention in corporate strategy formulation.'[22]

Is it any wonder that the Peter Principle exists where people rise to their level of incompetence? Worse still, managers are thrown in at the deep end, without a golden parachute and take years to develop leadership skills that could have been trained in a fraction of the time. These managers become stress-carriers, infecting those with whom they come into contact — and burnout is just around the corner. Economic suicide is the consequence of promoting 'Bob' or 'Mandla' because he's a nice guy and won't rock the boat — because it seemed like a good idea at the time!

'AN ARCHITECT NEEDS A PLAN' — TOWARD A MODEL OF LEADERSHIP

To develop people without a development model is tanta-mount to building a house without a foundation. To acquire and retain competent leaders, to let them know what they are expected to do, and to effectively utilise the organisation's human and other resources, people in organisations need models of leadership and management. We all carry models of our world, 'constructs' or 'mental maps' about good and bad, in our heads. Most of the time these are not made explicit although our assumptions, and prejudices cloud everything that we do.

An organisation cannot afford to have vague prejudices about leadership that have not been shown to be directly responsible for effective behaviour. If the specific competen-cies underpinning success are made overt and are tested, they can legitimately form the basis for future selection, promo-tion, development and allocation of rewards. A tried and tested model offers the most objective way of making 'human decisions' and indeed, for measuring performance.

An understanding of overt leadership competencies also takes away the defeating subjective arguments as to whether 'Nelson' is a good leader; or whether you agree with Buthelezi and whether indeed, we have a chance of creating a new, better South Africa. Any intelligent political discussion needs to be based on a model of effective leadership. The same applies to any professional who, by definition, is someone who has a model about their profession, knows how to carry out their duties and is consequently accountable for their actions.

This book is based on a model of effective leadership which has been derived from research concerning what leaders actually do. It has also been tempered by the realities, constraints and opportunities of application in a business context involving both a top-down and a bottom-up process of developing organisational leadership. Like any model, it is open to criticism and should always be subservient to what really works. In this respect I hope you will be challenged to develop your own 'model' of leadership which you subject to the test. Your future depends upon it.

SUMMARY

The following graphics, taken from my leadership competence programme, summarise 'the why' of leadership.

IS MANAGEMENT DEVELOPMENT A HOAX?
CEO Critical Success Factors

- Hard work
- Leadership
- Motivating 'people' and interpersonal issues
- Ability to learn on the job
- Link strategic planning and implementation

BUSINESS LEADERSHIP
The Vehicle to:

- Impact on skills shortage — develop/empower people
- Install hope-attractive vision of the 'New South Africa'
- Address reactive position of organisations to the turbulent environment of business
- Expanding expectations of the global workforce: Quality of life, participation, self expression
- Leadership — critical leverage point for organisational change (learning culture in a learning organisation)

CHAPTER II

✦

THE CHANGING CONTEXT
OF LEADERSHIP

Successful strategy involves the ability of an organisation to align itself with its external and internal environment in order to obtain sustainable competitive advantage. However, organisations confronted with exponential change and turbulence tend to retreat into technology, or become immobilised, rather than taking advantage of the situation with a creative response that involves building windmills before the hurricane arrives .[1]

Underpinning strategic leadership development is the changing nature of the organisation that any leader or potential leader must consider. Organisations must choose — to align themselves with the environment or to ignore it and become an immobilised ostrich with their head buried in the sand. However, the ostrich is destined to join the kwagga with more than its head buried.

Naisbet and Aburdene[2] list ways in which todays organisations are being reinvented (see the diagram on the following page). The global trend toward quality of life through ownership, autonomy and personal growth means that organisations that do not allow for expression of the human spirit will simply lose their best people. The question arises — how are organisations positioned to cope with these changes?

THE DEMISE OF THE HIERARCHICAL ORGANISATION.

The hierarchical model of organisations still predominates in the western world, as the primary method of organising people to achieve objectives. While this method of organisa-

15

REINVENTING THE ORGANISATION

- The best and brightest people gravitate to organisations fostering personal growth.
- Managers play the role of coach, teacher and mentor and facilitate on-the-job training.
- The best people want ownership (psychological and literal).
- Authoritarian management is yielding to democratic management (participation)
- Entrepreneurship and the development of new products is revitalising companies (learning organisation)
- Quality and autonomy are paramount.
- Intuition and creativity are challenging the 'all in the numbers' business school philosophy
- Large corporations are emulating the positive and productive qualities of small business.
- There is a shift toward third-party contractors and specialists.
- The workforce is focusing on quality-of-life issues.

tion served its purpose during the industrial revolution and war years, it is inadequate to cope with exponential change and the aspirations and productivity of people in a competitive environment .

These hierarchies are contrary to the basic human drive to learn, to find work meaningful, and to express creativity, responsibility and competence.

The rate at which an organisation learns and the development of individual ability to learn, will be its only source of competitive advantage in the 90' s and beyond.[3] Consequently, any structure and attitude that undermines learning contributes directly to the death of the organisation.

The hierarchical organisation expresses itself in authority relationships, rigid and time consuming decision making structures and the 'do's' and the 'do nots' included in job descriptions designed not to compliment the person but for the person to fit into.

Fundamental to this structure, rests a control-orientation to power operating from a win-lose orientation rather than an 'expandable pie' framework, which is the basis for the learning organisation. Deming summarises the impact of this thinking on the quality of an organisation's human resources:

'The prevailing system of management has destroyed our people. People are born with intrinsic motivation, self esteem, dignity, curiosity to learn, joy in learning. The forces of destruction being with toddlers — a prize for the best Halloween costume . . . grades in school, gold stars — and on up through university. On the job people, teams, divisions are ranked — rewards for the one at the top, punishment for the one at the bottom . . . causing further loss, unknown and unknowable.

'Instead the job of management in education, industry and government should be with optimisation of a system (not its fragmentation into management by objectives, and business plans put together division by division).[4]

This comment is indicative of a leadership and management crisis at every level of society. Given the imperative of the development of a country's human resources, the importance

of leaders that create organisations allowing for the expression of human potential and the accelerating of learning, cannot be overemphasised.

GROWING PEOPLE AND GROWING ORGANISATIONS

'If you want one year of prosperity, grow grain
If you want ten years of prosperity grow a tree
If you want one hundred years of prosperity grow people'[5]

On a national level, the need to develop people to their full
potential and the importance of addressing quality of life
issues is underscored in the De Lange Report of 1981. This
report looks to practical guidelines for the future education of
South Africans with a view to:

1. Promoting the actualisation of the potential of its inhabi-
    tants
2. Promoting the economic growth rate of the Republic of
    South Africa
3. Improving the quality of life of its inhabitants[6]

The only way to stay ahead in the learning race, and to meet
the needs and expectations of your people for quality of life,
participation and personal growth, is for the leader to take on
a developmental role. Given the escalating skills shortage, a
fundamental task of every leader is to grow people and grow
organisations where the human harvest can be cultivated. In
many organisations this will require a fundamental change in
the attitude of the 'sower of seeds'.

A FUNDAMENTAL SHIFT OF MIND

On an organisational level, Karl Hofmeyr comments that too
many advancement programmes consist of training programmes which candidates are asked to attend, in the hope
that at the end they will be ready for promotion. He points
out that most of what a person learns at work is on the job,

particularly from a superior. Consequently, the manager's training skills and attitude toward developing people are crucial, because the rewards and sanctions for behaviour are located in the department.[7]

Complimentary line managers' attitudes and skills are vital in helping to overcome feelings of inferiority, marginality and an external locus of control amongst potential black managers. Effective development and empowerment will only take place to the extent that people are able, willing and allowed to utilise their skills and potential.[8] This necessitates exploring the manager's attitude to power and its reciprocal — empowerment.

Creating and coping with change requires a belief from leader and subordinate alike, that they can effect change and exercise power to the benefit of themselves and the organisation.

Dr Jay Hall, chief advisor on manpower matters to President George Bush of America, points out that transformational leadership can only occur with a paradigm shift in the way leaders see the inherent potential of their followers:

'Managers have a distorted view of the people they manage. Fewer than twenty percent of managers today manage as if their workers are competent. Yet realistically, very little that managers do would have any relevance at all if it were not for one basic fact: by and large: *people are capable of doing what needs to be done.*'[9]

In respect of the above, productivity problems are of our own making in the sense that people perform as they are expected to perform.

Leadership involves a paradigm shift from viewing employees as children to creating adult expectations in an environment which offers meaningful work and involvement as the way to access human potential. In order to understand this power struggle and to affect change in this regard to the benefit of managers, followers and the organisation, the human dynamics underpinning power need to be understood.

Power is implicit in all human interactions — familial, sexual, occupational, national and international — either covertly or overtly.

Traditionally, society has had a negative view of power, a dislike for the authoritarian personality, of conflict in general and for manipulation of any kind. David McClelland distinguishes between primitive power and socialised power. The former operates from a win/lose orientation, where people are seen as pawns, and the focus is on maintaining the status quo.[10]

In contrast, socialised power (the positive side of power) sees people as origins of action, inherently capable and striving towards common goals through a shared vision that facilitates group strength and competence. In this respect, leadership has to find a balance between expressing personal dominance and the more socialised power or, put differently, to contend with the paradox between initiating change while being aware of people's desires.

Every leader must come to terms with power or the capacity to translate intention into reality and to sustain it. Transformative leadership is the wise use of this power, and while vision is the commodity of leaders, power is their currency.

Traditional management thinking promotes the idea that power is a fixed sum: if I have more, you have less. Managers who hold this view are archaic as it seriously retards getting extraordinary things done.

People who feel powerless, be they managers or subordinates, tend to hoard whatever shreds of power they have and tend to adopt petty and dictatorial management styles. Powerlessness creates organisational systems where political skills become essential and 'covering yourself' and 'passing the buck' become the preferred style for handing interdepartmental differences.[11]

Alternatively, the 'expandable pie' concept of power of giving power to get power — leads to greater reciprocity of influence. The leader and follower are willing to be mutually influenced by one another.

Leadership from a transformational perspective sees everyone as a potential leader with the focus being to enable others to act through fostering collaboration and strengthening people.[12] This involves competencies such as the effective use of power, developing others, and the ability to cope with and initiate change from both the leader and the follower. The leader then becomes a catalyst for growth through attention to structured development opportunities for followers, and in the expectations and manner in which he/she interacts with people.

Empowering others is simply a matter of enlightened self interest. Research indicates that when the leaders share power with other people, those people in turn feel more strongly attached to the leader and more committed to effectively carrying out their duties and responsibilities: they feel that a failure to carry out tasks lets themselves down as well as the boss.

> 'When you strengthen others, your level of influence with them is increased. When you go out of your way on behalf of others — you build up credit with them. By strengthening others, you place yourself on the subordinate's side'[13]

Clearly then, an axiom behind the effective development of subordinates is the acceptance of the responsibility by leaders to develop and empower people.

SUMMARY

This chapter has looked at ways in which today's organisations are being reinvented, particularly with respect to the needs and aspirations of people around the world. Those organisations that ignore the demand for quality of life and personal growth do so at their peril.

The hierarchical organisation is badly positioned to cope with these changes and is threatened with extinction as it is unable to cope with the learning race essential for corporate survival. The learning race is in turn dependent on the human race — a race to empower people and organisations.

Learning and empowerment requires a fundamental shift of mind — from seeing people as incompetent and operating from a win/lose orientation to seeing people as inherently capable and therefore sharing power. The 'expandable pie' concept of power in turn results in the leader, followers and organisation all 'winning'. These contrasting attitudes to power also indicate to a large extent the difference between being a leader and being a manager, which will be discussed in the next chapter.

✦
LEADERS OR MANAGERS?

INTRODUCTION

The debate concerning the difference between leadership and management has raged for some time. I have attempted to synthesise and condense the literature describing these differences.

It is important to point out that the leadership/management debate is not an either/or. Both activities are necessary. However, if organisations do not have sufficient leaders in addition to managers, they will simply not survive the nineties. Why? Because leadership is the central ingredient to the way progress is created and to the way organisations develop and survive in a changing environment. Consequently, I believe we should be talking about leadership development, rather than simply focusing on 'management development'.

Management and leadership are interdependent although people at every level of the organisation are increasingly being called on to be leaders in their own right.

Every person is required to take responsibility for growing and developing their own job and to find better ways of meeting consumer needs — whether this is sweeping the floor more efficiently and effectively or developing state of the art products. Leadership activity is therefore any activity that involves facilitating *productive behaviour* — as defined by both the organisation *and* its people. Show me a productive workforce, and you will discover a leader in their midst.

Review of the literature

The seminal work in distinguishing between traditional management and transformational leadership was undertaken by Zaleznik in 1977.[1] He elaborated on the difference according to a number of dimensions or categories, which will be discussed below.

A manager essentially sees goals as occurring due to external circumstances[2] and changing events and consequently reacts to circumstances after they have occurred due to an external locus of control.[3] Consequently, managers focus on the present — administering and maintaining systems in the focus or getting the task done correctly.[4] The instinct for survival[5] leads to a reliance on proven tools of planning and budgeting and a tendency to conserve affairs. This stability orientation tends to rely upon routine rather than interpersonal involvement which may produce unpredictable change. This would lead to a tendency to rely on positional power and to operate from a premise of viewing people as incompetent, and therefore not to be trusted.[6] Development of staff in terms of the managers win/lose power orientation is not a priority.

In contrast, a leader is someone who operates from an active attitude towards goals and, as part of self management,[7] sees themself as a source of action, by employing systems thinking.[8] A leader has a clear vision of the future and is active in influencing and guiding people while creating a context that is meaningful for others.[9] This presupposes the ability to empathise with people[10] while trusting and relying on others because they are viewed as creative and competent.[11] Consequently, the leader adopts the active role of teacher and creates a learning culture[12] together with the removal of organisational obstacles hindering personal growth in others — a prerequisite to empowerment. Fundamentally, the leader as pacemaker risks conflict as an inte-

gral part of individual and organisational growth, as opposed
to the manager as a peacemaker who avoids contentious
issues.[13]

A leader has the courage of his/her convictions and links
efficiency with effectiveness by facing fundamental issues
preventing organisational growth. This concern with effectiveness through people is elaborated on by Bennis and
Nanus:

> 'The problem with many organisations and especially the ones that are
> failing, is that they tend to be overmanaged and underled. This is the
> profound difference between management and leadership and both are
> important. Managers are people who do things right and leaders are
> people who do the right things right.'[14]

The following table summarises the difference between
leadership and management.

Table 3.1
LEADERSHIP vs MANAGEMENT

Category	Management	Leadership
Change	• Peacemakers — mainten-ance work, sustaining the present • Repeats and follows what is desirable and necessary • Administers • Maintains • First order change	• Pacemakers — fostering change and creating the future • Changes the way people think about what is desirable, possible and necessary • Innovates • Develops • Second order (fundamental change)
People	• Relies on systems	• Relies on people
Attention	• Does things right	• Does the right things right
Planning	• Thinks of today	• Strategic thinking — day after tomorrow

Category	Management	Leadership
Thinking	• Focus on present • Focus on getting things done • Events (reactive)	• Vision of the future and strategy to get there • Systemic structure — patterns underlying behaviour
Role	• Bringing about, implementing • Dressmaker • Pupil • 'You serve me'	• Influencing, guiding • Designer (vision, social architecture) • Teacher (more insightful views of reality; challenging assumptions) • Steward (attitude of serving others)
Attitude to Goals	• Impersonal, if not passive attitude. • Goals arise out of necessity. • External locus of control. • Responds to change. • Expectations ('You owe me').	• Active attitude to goals. • Influencing and changing organisation. • Internal locus of control • Exercise personal choice and responsibility for change and creating the future. • Aspirations ('I can create')
Meaning	• Respond to meaning	• High degree of personal meaning. • Manage and create meaning.
Work	• Reliant on planning, budgeting and other tools of management. • Instinct for survival dominates need for risk.	• Prepared to invest faith in others, excitement, risk opportunity. • Faith in key executive's judgement. • Focus on meaning as the foundation of motivation
Inter-personal	• Maintains low level of emotional involvement, task oriented.	• Ability to empathise — send and receive feedback

Category	Management	Leadership
Sense of self	• Sees self as conservative regulator of an existing order of affairs with which he/she personally identifies.	• Sense of self does not depend on membership, work roles or social indicators of identity. • Seeks opportunity for change.
Motivation	• Threat — 'Big Stick' • Rewards —'Carrots'	• Develops intrinsic motivation • Creates purpose/hope
Power	• Win/lose orientation • Relies on control	• Expandable-pie orientation • Gives power to get power • Counts on trust

CHAPTER IV

WHAT IS LEADERSHIP?

INTRODUCTION

There is widespread agreement that the successful organisation has one major attribute that sets it apart from unsuccessful organisations: dynamic and effective leadership.

There is also consensus that effective leaders are the scarcest resource of any business enterprise.[1] There is, however, little agreement concerning what exactly constitutes leadership competence.

Ask people what they think makes a good leader and invariably they will answer with a vague notion of 'charisma'. When pressed to explain they find difficulty in moving from subjective experiences to explaining specific behavioural characteristics that can be observed, trained and consequently evaluated. In other words, how can leadership be defined in a way that is useful for organisations and the training of leadership behaviour?

This chapter will present a brief overview of leadership theory from the 'personality trait approach' to the current transformational leadership which includes the competence approach underpinning this book. Thereafter the methodology and results of my South African leadership research will be discussed — arriving at the core competencies underpinning leadership excellence.

IT'S ALL IN THE GENES?

For centuries the notion was held (and still persists today) that leadership was exercised by the 'great men' who had been born with genetic qualities, rather than having learnt and been developed for that role. In 1924 Allport suggested nineteen 'essential' traits including 'intelligence' and 'erect aggressive carriage'.[2] However traits which correlated with success in one situation failed to do so in another, and no consistent pattern emerged.[3]

Recent research by Bennis and Nanus involving over ninety leaders in different professions found that the only common characteristic was the fact that all leaders were married.[4] Some were charismatic and some weren't, some were short, tall, thin, fat . . .

The 1950's saw the introduction of the leadership styles approach. An assumption underlying this approach was that there was one best style of leadership, favouring the democratic approach over the 'laissez-faire' and autocratic leader.[5] Extensive research, however, showed that the appropriateness of the style was dependent on the situation, maturity and needs of the followers. Further criticism was levelled at the exclusive focus on the leader without consideration being given to task and situational variables.[6]

The late 1960's saw leadership research concentrating on the situation and context of the leader. Fiedler identified three major situational factors which determine the appropriateness of a given leadership style. He focussed on the quality of leader/member relations, the degree of task structure, and the positional power of the leader.[7] The strength of the model appears to lie in the close relationship of the above factors, but it offers no diagnostic criteria for subordinates. The model, furthermore, assumes that the leadership process lies with one person only.[8]

Hersey and Blanchard[9] developed the commercially popular 'Situational Leadership Model' which suggested a life-cycle of leadership in which the degree of task and relationship behaviour exhibited by the leader must be analysed in conjunction with follower or subordinate maturity. In order for leaders to develop followers to their full potential, they must be able to vary their behaviour. This includes utilising various degrees of directive and supportive behaviour as subordinates move backwards or forwards along the maturity/immaturity continuum. The major strength of this approach is the developmental focus lacking in other models. However, the model has been criticised as being simplistic.[10] Training in a South African context has also tended to focus more on the identification, rather than on the job application of leadership style.

Chris Argyris focussed primarily on the attitudes and underlying assumptions or mental beliefs of the leader as the critical ingredient of change. The strength of this model is the emphasis on challenging attitudes underpinning behaviour and developing new 'paradigms' of the world.[11] He developed an in-depth learning experience for leaders, which requires implementation by a highly skilled facilitator, and is consequently limited in its application.

The new theories of leadership evolved in reaction to the increasingly sophisticated models which became difficult to implement. This 'back to the basics' approach focussed primarily on what leaders *do in practice* in order to be effective. The new theories of leadership stress the importance of leaders in transforming their followers to leaders and elevating people by building commitment through meaning.[12]

The focus on transformational leadership takes on enormous significance in light of South Africa's increasing skills shortage and productivity problems.

NEW THEORIES OF LEADERSHIP

Dissatisfaction with the relevance of previous theories of leadership, and as a result of changing environmental conditions and worker expectations, the late 1970' s and 1980' s saw the emergence of a number of new leadership theories. These tended to focus on what leaders do in order to be effective.

These approaches represent a fundamental shift in the way people are motivated,[13] the way the leader sees and relates to followers,[14] and the manner in which change is viewed.[15] The overt competence approach, based on what recognised leaders do in order to transform and empower their followers, is based on extensive research both internationally[16] and locally within South Africa.[17, 18]

The above approach formed the starting point of my research. In addition, the work of Bennis and Nanus, Kouzes and Posner, Boyatsis, Limmerick, Ball and Ashbury, Senge, Carkhuff, Peters, Manning and Falkenburg was drawn on as a basis to compile the leadership competence questionnaire. A summary of these authors and how they complement and expand the original model of Bennis and Nanus is included at the end of the chapter. (Table IV:I)

LEADERSHIP DEFINED

Numerous authors comment on the difficulty in defining leadership, stating that it is easier to define and recognise what it is not. Tom Peters defines leadership as:

A unique alliance between managers and workers that fully engages the talents and potential of everyone in the organisation.'[19]

Bennis and Nanus emphasise the importance of fostering creative change through a vision by creating a meaningful work context, communicating the vision, developing trust, and effectively managing yourself — thereby empowering subordinates. Peter Senge places emphasis on the creation of learning organisations by emphasising vision, alignment of purpose and personal mastery and responsibility to effect change. For the purposes of this book, leadership encompasses all the above and is defined as:

'The competencies and processes required to enable and empower ordinary people to do extraordinary things in the face of adversity, and constantly turn in superior performance to the benefit of themselves and the organisation.'

Empowerment, like leadership, is a much used and little understood concept. Linda Human[20] sees empowerment as the process of developing subordinates who are able (competent), willing (motivated) and allowed (authority and responsibility) to use their full potential in discharging their responsibiities at work. Other authors emphasise the process of enhancing feelings of self efficacy among organisational members, through the identification of conditions that foster powerlessness and through their removal both by formal and organisational practices and informal techniques of providing efficacy information.[21]

For the purposes of this book empowerment is defined as:

'The act of investing and authorising, where people and organisations are enabled to achieve goals. This involves the sharing of power and authorising people to think and make decisions. Moreover, empowering emphasises skilling people in competencies needed to discharge their responsibilities and removing organisational obstacles hindering personal and organisational development.'[22]

LEADERSHIP AND COMPETENCE

The search for a model of management/leadership is complicated by a person's confusion between espoused theory and theory in use. Although managers do not always consciously follow a model during their daily activities, every managerial act, like research, rests on generalisations, assumptions and hypotheses. This study adopts a competence approach to identifying leadership which is shared by Bennis and Nanus

and the recent international trend focussing on the practices
of effective leaders in a work context.

Job competence is defined as: 'a set of generic characteristics expressed in motives, traits, self image, social rules,
knowlege and skills which may be apparent in many forms
of behaviour and different actions.'[23]

The emphasis underlying competence is on the application of knowledge and skills, representing a move away from
traditional testing instruments, such as the I.Q. test, measuring inherent potential. The competence approach represents
a shift from activities, roles and descriptive models to *results
and output* — based on models of excellence.[24] A major reason
for selecting the competence approach is that it provides a
causal link between a statement of competence and superior
performance by a leader.[25]

The foray into what McClelland called competence assessment, saw standardised tests of intelligence and aptitude as
crude instruments that may be irrelevant to real life success.
At that time McClelland concluded that:

> 'It seems wise to abandon the search for pure ability factors and select
> tests instead, that are valid, in the sense that scores on them change as
> the person grows in experience, wisdom and ability to perform effec-
> tively on various tasks that life presents him.'[26]

Tests should assess competencies involved in clusters-of-life
outcomes and should include not only occupational, but social outcomes, such as leadership and interpersonal skills.

The competence approach has been adopted by the
American Society for Training and Development and by the
South African Board for Personnel Practice who have developed a Generic Competency Model for Human Resource
practitioners.[27] The American Society for Training and Development made use of a theoretical appraisal of training, a
nominal group technique and competence questionnaire in
order to arrive at training and development competencies.[28]

A similar approach has been followed for the South African research, with a questionnaire being used to collect data in preference to the behavioural events interview used by Bennis and Nanus. The questionnaire was chosen because it was an objective of this research to validate a questionnaire that could be used with comparative ease in a number of different organisational settings in the future — a process that is less expensive and time consuming than the behavioural events interview.

Consequently:

❏ *Competence* is defined as 'the exhibition of specific behaviour and attitudes being clearly demonstrated and therefore measurable, and is distinguishable from the inherent potential to perform.'

❏ *Strategic Training and Development* is 'the identification of needed skills and active management of employee learning for the long-range future in relation to explicit corporate and business strategies.' This includes activities designed to ensure that the individuals are properly equipped to carry out jobs that fall into the management development category.[29]

❏ *Learning* — A person's ability to assimilate, conceptualise and *implement* knowledge, attitudes and skills in a comprehensive manner, leading to individual and organisational growth.

LEADERSHIP CAN BE DEVELOPED! 'AND SO SAY ALL OF THEM'

Gail Kelly introduced some ground-breaking work when she researched the skills necessary for success at Chief Executive Officer level, and the process whereby these can be cultivated. Her conclusions are drawn from interviews with twenty five CEO' s, each of whom is widely acknowledged as successful.

These leaders included Raymond Ackerman, Neal Chapman, Chris Ball, Vic Hammond, Robin Lee, Tony Norton, Myer Kahn, Bob Tucker, Peter Searle and Grant Thomas.

Several key insights have emerged from the study. The most significant of these relates to the importance, from the chief executive officer's point of view, of being in touch with one's people — of being able to communicate with them, empower them and draw them in behind one.

Also significant is the CEO's ability to understand the fundamental principles and processes of business (rather than just the technical aspects) and ability not only to cope with, but also to initiate change.

The research clearly reveals that leadership competencies *can* be developed. It also highlights the need for *relevant* management/leadership education in both the corporate and more formal university and business school settings. Kelly also points out that any development and growth needs to be based on a *generic model of success* that is common to all exceptional leaders regardless of context.[30] However, most organisations do not have a strategic development plan, or a tried-and-tested model of expressed competence underpinning excellence. Consequently, training cannot be shown to impact significantly on an organisation's bottom line.

The South African leadership study that I conducted in 1991, was designed to begin providing a model of leadership competence which had been tried and tested on a strategic and operational level.

TOWARD A VALID SOUTH AFRICAN LEADERSHIP MODEL

The purpose of the South African research was to identify competencies within a major South African company from both the leader and the follower perspectives. The leadership competence model of Bennis and Nanus (1985), emanating from comprehensive research — involving ninety effective leaders in the U.S.A., was used as a basis to distinguish excellent from average leadership activity in order to assess its relevance within the South African context[31] In terms of the above model, the dual perspective of the leader and the led, and its focus on overt competencies, is unique to South Africa.

The South African company comprises twenty eight strategic business units, including world class companies in their own right and involved in a diverse range of business and service activity.

Of the original ninety leaders in the U.S.A., sixty of these were from business, with the remainder including leaders from across the political spectrum, orchestra leaders, film producers, athletes, coaches and others.

The researchers stress that there seemed to be no obvious pattern for their respondents' success. Personalities, physical characteristics, managerial styles all differed. Yet, by careful probing and syntheses of data, the researchers were able to isolate four areas of competency; four types of human handling skills that they believed applied to all ninety of their participants. These they called 'strategies'.

The four strategies identified included:
❑ The management of attention through vision.
❑ The management of meaning through communication.
❑ Trust.
❑ The management of self.

The four competencies are interdependent and build on each other and thus effective leadership, must display *all four elements* as they are generally sequential. First, leaders need to capture people's attention through an inspiring vision of the future. This then needs to be communicated through the organisation to ensure common 'views' of reality, and to motivate people. Trust is essential in order to commit people to action, particularly in adverse circumstances. These three strategies are in turn dependent on the leaders' self management, or ability to accept responsibility for personal action and change. In addition, he/she must have an awareness of inappropriate actions and independently alter these in terms of organisational objectives.

The South African research elaborated on these four strategies by breaking them down into competence statements which better describe each activity. In addition, a fifth competence was added — that of empowerment — which, the literature suggests, is a fundamental role of the leader.

In all, twenty five competency statements were designed in order to offer useful specific guidelines for leadership implementation (and are included at the end of each chapter, describing the above competencies).

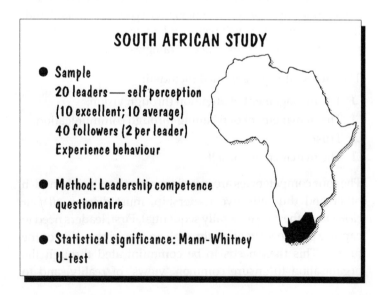

SOUTH AFRICAN STUDY

- Sample
  20 leaders — self perception
  (10 excellent; 10 average)
  40 followers (2 per leader)
  Experience behaviour

- Method: Leadership competence
  questionnaire

- Statistical significance: Mann-Whitney
  U-test

THE SAMPLE

The leadership sample consisted of twenty of the most senior people in a large South African organisation. Each person was a leader in his own right, heading up a diverse range of services and businesses. They therefore had a leadership role both within their organisations (to employees) and in their consulting capacity (to stakeholders).

The leadership group was then split into two — ten excellent and ten average leaders, chosen on the basis of performance-appraisal ratings, subordinate ratings of the leaders and peer ratings at the same level of the organisational hierarchy. The better the cumulative ratings, the more likely people were to be allocated the excellent label.

Immediately below the leaders in the organisational hierarchy, a random sample of forty subordinates was drawn, two per leader. A self-administered questionnaire was developed, comprising twenty five single concept statements describing overt measurable leadership behaviour. Leaders were asked to fill in a self-rating questionnaire, while followers rated their leader's behaviour. This allowed comparison between the two groups of leaders and the two 'excellent' and 'average' groups of followers.

Followers were guaranteed anonymity and leaders did not even know who had been chosen in the random sample, as initially all followers immediately below the leader were asked to rate their boss. This allowed for the following *objectives* to be realised:

1. *To identify South African leader competencies that distinguish effective from average performers.*
2. *To clarify how these correspond with an international study. It is hypothesised that there will be a high degree of similarity in that leadership competencies are considered generic as the original study was run across a number of leadership contexts, such as businessmen, politicians, church and sportsmen.*

It was hypothesised that:

1. *There will be a significant difference between leaders self-ratings and follower ratings of the leaders between the excellent and average leader sample.*

2. *The perceptions of excellent leaders and their followers will be relatively congruent. This will be expressed through comparative mean scores and a significantly lower 'gap differential' than the average sample.*

3. *Followers of excellent leaders will feel significantly more empowered than followers of average leaders. Empowerment, therefore, is both a consequence and a competence of effective leadership.*

Results from the questionnaire allowed for the identification of specific behaviours distinguishing excellent from average leadership — from both a self and a follower perspective.

RESEARCH DESIGN/METHODOLOGY

A self administered questionnaire was developed from an exhaustive literature search concerning the application of the four leadership competencies described by Bennis and Nanus, as well as previous leadership research and theory concerning empowerment and its relationship to leadership (See Table IV:I overleaf.) As previously described, empowerment has been added to the four competencies because it was hypothesised as being a specific competence or strategy that all excellent leaders consciously express in addition to the other aforementioned competencies.

Twenty five single concept statements, five per competency, were developed and placed in random order throughout the questionnaire.

The structure of the questionnaire allowed for the analysis of results on a number of levels, thereby confirming the above hypotheses. This was piloted and altered accordingly on five leaders and five subordinates who were not included in the random samples. Two covering letters were attached to questionnaires depending on the leader/follower category, explaining the purpose, rationale, confidentiality and benefits of completing the questionnaire. Clear instructions were attached, together with the importance of completing all questions.

The questionnaire statements were measured on a nine point ordinal scale. A score of 1 indicated that leadership 'activity was not expressed', 5 — a moderately frequent expression of activity, and 9 — where 'activity was manifested in all situations'. The scale allows the comparison of competent behaviour on a number of levels.

For the purposes of comparing the two groups (mean scores), and to compute the perceptual gap analysis, the assumption was made that the scale behaves in an interval fashion. Runyon and Haber point out that although it is debatable that many scales achieve interval measurement, most behavioural scientists are willing to make the assumption that they do.[32]

LIMITATIONS

The focus of this research is on a large South African company that plays a major leadership role with respect to its customers through twenty eight diverse service functions. For this reason, results may not be precisely applicable to other organisations which would necessitate controlling for organisational and industry effect. The identified competencies do, however, offer a model of South African leadership that can be tried, tested and adapted to meet your organisation's needs.

Table 4.1:
LEADERSHIP STRATEGIES/APPROACHES

LIMMERICK	KELLY C.E.O. SUCCESS FACTORS	BALL & ASBURY	BOYATSIS MANAGERIAL COMPETENCE	KOUZES & POSNER
• Loosely coupled systems handle change more effectively • Collaborative individualism	• Ability to cope with and initiate change • Leadership is a process • In touch and empower people	• Leader key to successful company • Team that hums • Training	• Effective use of power • Developing others	• Leadership is a process — not a position • Enabling others to act – foster collaboration – strengthen others
• Use of language, knowledge, symbols • Manager of meaning — mission	• Communicate	• Communicate	LEADERSHIP CLUSTER • Logical thought • Diagnostic use of concepts	• Inspiring common purpose – envision the future – enlist others
• Vision • Mission • Identity • Culture	• Communicate • Understand fundamental principles and processes of business	• Vision creates meaning	GOAL AND ACTION MANAGEMENT • Efficiency orientation • Proactivity • Conceptualisation	• Inspiring a vision • Challenging the process – search for opportunities – experiment and take risks
• Autonomous delegated authority — empower the individual • Openly shared goals, values for collaborative action	• Being in touch with people • Interpersonal skills • Warmth/candour • Put people in position to achieve goals	• Encourage the head and heart	HUMAN RESOURCE MANAGEMENT CLUSTER • Positive regard for others • Managing group process	• Encouraging the heart – recognise individual contributions – Celebrate accomplish-ments
• Protective, individualistic, politically aware • Empathy • Change skills • Networking • Personal mastery	• Competencies can be developed • Look out for new challenges • Prepared to risk • Confidence and faith in own judgement • Love to work • Learning	• Energy • Initiative • 'Coal-face' MBWA • Work is play	• Accurate self-assessment • Self Control • Stamina • Concern with Impact • Self confidence • Spontaneity	• Modelling the way – set example – plan small wins • Credible, honest, competent, inspiring

BENNIS & NANUS	SENGE	CARKHUFF	PETERS	MANNING	FALKENBURG
AUTHORS CENTRAL FOCUS Empowering others	• Systems thinking • Personal mastery • Team learning • Mental models • Vision	• Empowering the creative leader (everyone) • Processors of information	• Everyone is a leader • Change central to growth • Growing leaders	• Leader as change agent • Recruit and train competencies • Leadership a scarce resource • Empowerment	• Leadership — creating challenge out of change • Focus on spiritual resources
Management of meaning Communicate	• Focus on mission • Fundamental causes • Alignment	• Centralise by mission	• Work teams	• Communicate vision	• Provides meaning and purpose
Management of attention Vision	• Building shared vision • Creating tension — vision and current reality	• Critical Mass • Thinking and planning skills • Entre-preneurial • Intro-preneurial	• Vision and values	• Align behind common objectives • Focus on fundamentals	• Reduce stress • Fundamental principles and ultimate values (truth, justice, love, dignity, quality) • Service, quality, integrity, growth
Management of trust	• Tell the truth • Enrolment • Leaders as 'servant / steward'	• Situational empathy • *Interpersonal Skills* • Attend • Respond • Personalise • Initiate	• Ownership	• Relies on people	• Merge individual and organisational excellence • Empathy
Management of Self	• Personal mastery • Improve mental models • Challenge belief systems	• Develop creative thinkers • Move from conditioned responders to 'processors' of information	• Self esteem • Continuous learning • Empower-ment	• Foster change • Understand Human Nature • Tolerate ambiguity and accept responsibility • Gut feel	• View change as opportunity • Courage, toughness / focus on human principles • Patience and understanding

ANALYSIS AND FINDINGS

The structure of the questionnaire allowed for the analysis of results on a number of levels, thereby confirming the studies' hypotheses.

The raw data was analysed using the Man-Whitney U test, a non-parametric test illustrating the significant difference between groups — or the excellent and average leadership samples. Comparisons were made between the composite groups, leader self scores and follower scores on the 25 competence statement (five per competency) in order to substantiate the hypotheses.

The following points summarise the findings of the research:

1. Excellent leaders were rated significantly higher (*by their followers*) on the dimensions of the management of attention, meaning, trust and self.

2. There was no difference between excellent leader *self scores* and average leader self scores on the above dimensions.

3. Consequently, follower perceptions of leadership become the crucial variable in identifying leadership competence. Leader self-rating is not a good indicator of leadership competence.

4. As expected from the above, the perceptions of excellent leaders and their followers are more congruent than those in the average sample.

5. The empowerment of followers by excellent leaders also emerged as a distinguishing competence of effective leadership. This has major implications for the leader's role in impacting on an organisation's skills shortage. No formal training and/or organisational developmental efforts will be successful unless attention is simultaneously given to developing leadership competence.

These findings are diagramatically summarised opposite.

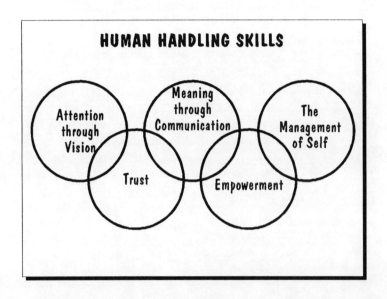

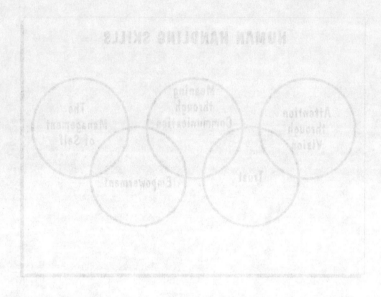

HUMAN HANDLING SKILLS

- The Management of Self
- Meaning through Communication
- Attention through Vision
- Empowerment
- Trust

PERCEPTIONS
- Leader self perception not a good indicator
- Follower perception is the key variable

CHAPTER V

ATTENTION THROUGH VISION

INTRODUCTION

Vision is part of every businessperson's vocabulary — but judging from the underperformance of most companies, it is easier said than applied. Articles and videotapes on the subject abound, proclaiming 'The Way' towards prosperity. In part the problem lies with the 'pop psychology' quick-fix package approach proclaiming ten steps to success, without understanding the complex human dynamics underpinning change, or the rationale behind visionary behaviour.

Vision is not a product of psychotic behaviour, nor something that happens to people riding a donkey on the road to Damascus. Although Paul no doubt underwent a transformational experience, and many a business would welcome divine intervention, there is no guarantee that God would choose YOU as one of the favoured few when the opposition has similar prayers.

CREATING THE FUTURE

A vision is simply a picture, target or goal of the future that is realistic, credible and consequently better than the present. Many of us are prisoners of the past and fixated by the present. In this respect, we are victims of past failures and unworked — through experiences as well as desire for instant gratification supplied by the hire purchase and fast food industries.

However, we had better pay attention to our future because that is where 'hope that springs eternal in the human breast' resides and pulls us forward, because we believe in what lies ahead. Leadership, and indeed success, on every human level, is dependent on a positive vision or hope of our future.

Problems of the present often seem so overwhelming that it seems pointless to talk about the future. And yet the time to sow the seeds of our future is exactly in the hard times. However difficult, it is vital to lift our heads to look beyond the present circumstances that demand our attention and consume our energy.

VICTOR FRANKL — VISION AMIDST DEATH

'He who has a why, can withstand any what.'[1]

Victor Frankl, the famous Austrian psychiatrist, is set apart from many of his medical and psychological colleagues in that most of his work emanates from his personal experiences in a German concentration camp. There he discovered the essence of survival and motivation under the worst possible human conditions.

From those people who survived, Frankl found a common thread — they all had something significant yet to do in their future. For one person it was to finish a series of books that only he could complete, for another, his child who was waiting for him in a foreign country. Once people were reminded of their future, they were empowered to survive.

The choice of looking to the future worked for Frankl too. He forced his thoughts to turn from his inward pre-occupation with food, and constant fear of the gas chambers to another subject.

'I saw myself standing on the platform of a well-lit, pleasant and warm lecture room. In front of me sat an attentive audience on soft, upholstered chairs. I was giving a lecture on the psychology of the concentration camp. By this method I succeeded in somehow rising above the situation and suffering of the moment. And I observed them (the suffering and guards) as if they were of the past.'[2]

These experiences point out the primacy of each person having something yet to accomplish in the future. Frankl concludes in his book, *'Man's Search for Meaning'* that 'It is a peculiarity of man that he can only live by looking to the future. And this is his salvation even in the most difficult moments of his existence.'

The challenge then facing every leader is to create a vision of the future that beckons each person in the organisation to commit themselves to action. A second and equally important task is to *create a context* where this human need can be realised and in which people are enabled to contribute to realising that future.

VISION — A NATIONAL IMPERATIVE

Joel Barker, in his videotape 'The Power of Visions', points out that a positive vision of the future is one of the strongest motivations for change that people possess.[3] Barker cites the work of Fred Polak, who on surveying the literature of nations both ancient and present, found that a significant vision *preceded* success on a national scale.

In example after example, firstly a compelling image of the future was offered by leaders. That image was then shared by a community and they agreed to support it. Then together, acting in concert, they went about actualising the vision.

This was as true for Greece 2 500 years ago as it is today where we see the power of vision sweeping across the world from eastern Europe to the Pacific rim. Many of these nations, as they began their climb to greatness, did not have the right resources or obvious strategic advantage. Instead they had a profound vision of their own future.

The message is clear to South Africa as politicians gather around the negotiating table to thrash out our future. Forget about the economic debate of nationalisation vs capitalism or the percentages and decimal points required for a positive growth rate. Start instead to build a powerful vision of the future to which all South Africans can commit themselves — and then invest time, money and energy to develop leaders who can enable ordinary people to do extraordinary things in the face of adversity. The fuel for growth on any level is the creation of leadership that can empower people and unleash human potential in creating their own future.

A national vision needs to be more specific than 'a new South Africa', but sufficiently broad to reach people in every socio-economic group. Its detail needs to spell out the what, how, when, why and where so that people are pulled forward and a space is created in which each person can participate in the actualising of this vision. The message is clear: nations with a vision of their own future are powerfully enabled. Those without vision are at risk.

LEADERSHIP AND VISION

The competence of vision has two essential purposes: firstly, the creation of an attractive future that motivates people and enables individuals to find their own roles within the organisation; and which helps people to engage in a creative and purposeful venture.

And secondly, to get people's *attention* and to provide a sense of focus as to where the organisation is going. This allows both the leader and the follower to make choices in terms of their time and activity, and consequently to distribute decision-making widely.

A vision provides focus concerning the central purpose of the organisation, and equally important, transmits unbridled clarity of what is expected from employees. Under these conditions the human energies of an organisation are *aligned* toward a common end, rather than being fragmented. The leader, by focussing attention on the *emotional and spiritual resources* of the organisation and its values and operations, engenders *commitment rather than compliance*. The manager by contrast, operates on the physical resources of the organisation, on its capital, human skills, raw materials and technology.

Although leaders are constantly aware of what they want (and are extremely result-orientated) the vision itself is not expressed in financial terms — which is always a consequence of the vision. For example, the idea of creating a leadership learning centre that will equip present and future African leaders with competencies that directly impact on organisational growth and productivity — is the vision. It is in the striving for and realising of this vision, that wealth (both financial and emotional) will be created. Consequently, the focus is on adding value to society through growing leaders — and not to make money. The vision can be as vague as a dream, or as precise as a goal or mission statement — as long as it serves the original purpose — to get people's attention and to focus this attention on the future in a way that energises people.

WHERE DOES THE VISION COME FROM?

A valid criticism directed at many organisations stems from a 'Masterplan' that is designed by a select few and then imposed on people. The trend of the chosen few heading into the bush for a 'Bosberaad' to return with the vision or mission statement, is as foolish as it is undemocratic. People feel uninvolved in the process, and consequently 'the document' is filed away only to be looked at next year when the process begins again. Worse still, if you ask people what the purpose is of the organisation — they have to refer to the document itself rather than having internalised it.

The process of formulating the vision illustrates the difference between commitment and compliance. The vision does not originate from the leader personally, but from others, and in this sense is never truly original. John F. Kennedy spent a great deal of time reading history and studying the ideas of great thinkers, while Martin Luther King studied religious and ethical ideologies as well as the traditions of his own and other peoples.

A leader can seek guidance from the past (trends, history, experiences), the present (facing up to the real issues confronting the organisation), and the future (environmental trends impacting on the organisation). In addition, a leader must be guided both by his/her people and his/her customers. What are the dreams, aspirations and needs of the people in the organisation? Why do they choose to work at that organisation and what do they hope to achieve? What ideas do they have for growing and expanding their own departments? What do they want to do with their lives, professionally and personally? If employees and managers have not taken responsibility for their own vision of the future, the leader must challenge them to do so.

Ian McCrae, Eskom Chief Executive, comments on the importance of listening to and staying in touch with your people. 'There is no better way to know how well or badly you are doing than to ask your staff — and then to follow their advice.'[4] McCrae spends a great deal of time asking people's advice on his business practices and what they expect from him and the organisation in future, as well as people's own aspirations for their departments.

The leader must then accumulate these multi-visions and discern which information is important. It is in the incorporation of this information into the bigger picture, that the real art of leadership lies and the final choice of creating a new future rests. The leader draws on selecting, synthesising and articulating skills which must be formulated into an appropriate vision, combining both reason and intuition and articulating the desires of all stakeholders, including the personal visions of employees.

And so the Eskom vision of: 'The best performing power company in the world', 'electricity for all' and the 'creation of economic wealth through the provision of energy in Southern Africa' is sufficiently broad and encompassing for all employees to feel that they are contributing to a new, better South Africa.[5] It is also something that 'Mr Mpho Pitso' or 'Mary Radebe' can feel proud of when they go home at night and explain to relatives who do not have electricity that they are part of bringing 'light' into their worlds.

PRINCIPLES OF VISION

No discussion on leadership is complete without referring to Peter Senge and his seminal work, 'The Fifth Discipline.'[6] Senge points out that leadership starts with the principle of creative tension.

Creative tension comes from seeing clearly where we *want to be* (vision), and telling the truth about where we are, *our current reality*. The gap between the two generates a natural tension. Both components are essential in creating this tension, which can be resolved in two basic ways — by raising current reality towards the vision, or by lowering the vision toward current reality.

Both components of tension are critical in creating change. Many organisations spend their lives avoiding the *real issues* which hinder effective performance. Whether it is the elaborate psychological defence mechanisms employed to help the individual cope with reality, or the *abstraction* wars of the organisation, the nett result of avoiding the truth is the same — we continue to evoke self-defeating behaviour. We choose stability rather than change.

Alternatively, individuals and organisations very seldom have a clear picture of their future. Consequently, my con-

stant challenge to people is, whether in individual therapy or
corporate consulting, what do you want to create; where are
you going?

The reason leadership is such a scarce resource is because
the vast majority of people avoid confronting real issues and
do not take responsibility for choosing their own future. We
are afraid of choice because it involves responsibility and
commitment — where we have no one to blame for failure but
ourselves. The alternative of having a vague notion of something better — 'the gods willing' — is evidence of a victim
mentality that eventually breeds apathy.

Granted, there are always a multitude of restraining factors impinging on our future. However, it is not what happens
to us that creates problems but the way that we choose to
respond to life's knocks. Put differently, the only people that
don't have problems are in the cemetery. The critical difference between leaders and followers is that the former have
a clear vision of the future and are prepared to face current
reality or the truth about their own and the organisation's
restraining forces.

Leaders are also people with uncompromising standards
of excellence. However when the going gets tough, rather
than limit tension by dropping standards and settling for
mediocrity, leaders hold fast to their standards until current
reality rises to meet the vision and the vision becomes a
reality.

The natural energy for changing reality then comes from
holding a picture of what might be, which is more important
to people than what is. However vision without the understanding of current reality will more likely foster cynicism
than creativity — labelling you as 'a dreamer' without your
feet on the ground.

The message for business should be clear. It is pointless,
in the absence of a clear vision of the future of the organisation

that is known to everyone, simply to embark on a retrenchment exercise. People's motivation is dependent on understanding why retrenchment is necessary and how this fits in with the future of the organisation — if indeed it has a future. If there is no vision people will simply assume that there is no future and hence look for better alternatives (before abandoning ship). Likewise, cost cutting without an honest appraisal of factors which inhibit growth — such as declining customers and intransigent management attitudes that destroy human potential — will simply generate future problems. Consequently any 'belt tightening' exercise must *also* be accompanied with effective leadership that consciously motivates and empowers people. In essence, development *must* accompany cost cutting if the company is to survive long-term.

FROM THEORY TO PRACTICE

On a business level, Ian McCrae points out that people need to know where the organisation is going, and to constantly focus on bottom line issues, objectives and goals.[7] Jeff Liebesman of F.S.I. illustrates the importance of understanding current reality by listening to people at the coal-face who can often give you the best advice for implementing your job in that area. Leadership, says Liebesman, 'is about identifying a strategy that works and then getting people to believe in it. This involves helping people understand your vision and finally leading people into an active programme that works.'[8]

On a political level, Martin Luther King illustrates the importance of both vision and current reality in his famous 'I have a dream' speech:

'One hundred years later the life of the Negro is still sadly crippled by the manacles of segregation and the chains of discrimination. One hundred years later the Negro lives on a lonely island of poverty in the midst of a vast ocean of material prosperity. One hundred years later the Negro is still vanquished in the corners of American society, and finds himself in exile in his own land. So we have come here today to dramatise the shameful conditions; in a sense we have come to our nation's capital to cash a cheque.'

The cheque refers to 'cashing in' and actualising the Declaration of Independence to which all Americans fall heir — the riches of freedom and security of justice. However, counterbalancing the reality of Negro life is a vision of the future that *all* people can strive for:

'Let us not wallow in the valley of despair. I say to you today, my friends, even though we face the difficulties of today and tomorrow, I still have a dream. I have a dream that one day on the red hills of Georgia, the sons of former slaves and the sons of former slave owners will be able to sit down together at the table of brotherhood . . .

'I have a dream, that one day even the state of Mississippi — sweltering with the heat of injustice, sweltering with the heat of oppression, will be transformed into an oasis of freedom and justice. I have a dream that my four little children will one day live in a nation where they will be judged not by the colour of their skin but by the content of their character . . .

'I have a dream that one day every valley shall be exalted, every hill and mountain shall be made low, the rough places will be made plains and the crooked places will be made straight and the glory of the Lord shall be revealed and all flesh shall see it together.

'This is our hope, this is the faith that I go back to the South with. With this faith we will be able to hew out of the mountain of despair a stone of hope. With this faith we will be able to transform the jangling discords of our nation into a beautiful symphony of brotherhood. With this faith we will be able to work together, to pray together, to struggle together, to go to jail together, to stand up for freedom together, knowing that we will be free one day. This will be the day, when all of God's children will be able to sing with new meaning: my country 'tis of thee, sweet land of liberty, of thee I sing. Land where my fathers died, land of the pilgrim's pride, from every mountainside, let freedom ring.'[9]

King illustrates the fundamental role of the leader in managing and creating tension that will lead to vision attainment:

'Just as Socrates felt that it was necessary to create tension in the mind so that individuals could rise from the bondage of myths and half truths, so must we create the kind of tension in society that will help men rise from the dark depths of prejudice and racism.'[10]

Through a compelling vision it is indeed possible to create an environment where the lion will lie down with the lamb;

where the A.N.C., Inkatha and N.P. meet together and where managers and workers strive for similar goals. Leaders the world over, continuously need to look at current reality hindering organisational growth, while creating tension with a clear, attractive vision of the future, that like an elastic band, pulls people towards it.

ORGANISATIONAL VISION STARTS WITH INDIVIDUAL VISION

A fundamental role of the leader is to challenge individuals to create their own visions for the future of their business unit, department or specialist task.

The acid test of leadership is the presence of empowered people in organisations. Empowerment in turn depends on the belief that 'I can begin to create my own future'. This in turn presupposes an internal locus of control which places responsibility squarely on 'my shoulders' rather than externalising responsibility for change and blaming others — both below and above you in the organisation.

Leaders face an unenviable task of holding others accountable for their actions and allowing people to take consequences in this regard. The first step to stop people 'passing the buck' is to remove any real organisational obstacles (current reality) hindering professional development. Mutual expectations can be contracted with the person in a joint venture, where the leader agrees to create space for the person in an empowering environment, while the employee/follower agrees to deliver the goods in terms of excellent performance — based on his/her individual vision.

In this way people can no longer blame outside factors alone for poor performance, as the organisational consequences for not achieving are enforced. The difficult part is in creating an empowering environment which renders excuses invalid — and will be discussed later. The same principles of vision for organisational leadership then apply to individual growth and success. After all, the individual must learn to lead him/herself before he can lead others. The principles also underpin any sphere of human excellence.

An Olympic rowing crew needs to be constantly aware of the current reality or weak areas in their technique and psychological make-up that hold them back. Ignoring these in training will only expose them (during the race) under pressure. The crew need constantly to focus on their goal and to maintain standards of excellence to sustain them through the arduous training hours on the water. The performance of the Olympic crew is as good as the weakest person's individual vision — and the extent to which the vision is shared by all the rowers.

Nic Bester, the 1991 Comrades Marathon winner, illustrated the importance of creating tension between vision and current reality. He worked extensively with a psychologist in overcoming his physical and mental weakness during the last 20 km of the 90 km race. This included learning to overcome anxiety concerning the exhausting pain (current reality) by learning to relax and to visualise himself running strongly over the hardest part of the course. Nic took responsibility for creating his racing future prior to the event, which he hence won, running strongly over the last 20 km.

This illustrates the point that in the human race, when the spirit weakens, reinvesting the energy into your vision is the wisest alternative. In fact, it is the only alternative to creating your future.

INSTILLING HOPE AND COMMITMENT —
A FUNDAMENTAL ROLE OF LEADERSHIP

Ours is a society, says Anthony Campolo, that has caused us to lose our identity.[11] Each social group that we belong to — at work, the family, religious organisations, friends, sporting

and cultural groups and professional associations — defines
us differently.

Thus one of the most pressing questions in our society is
— Who am I? The self, says Compolo, is not waiting to be
discovered through introspection. The self is waiting to be
created through commitment. It is commitment to a cause, a
future, a goal, that creates identity. Without commitment we
are hollow men, the straw people, blown to and fro by the
wind.

Every human being must decide what it is that has ulti-
mate significance and how best to express this commitment
in a work and social context. The people who have a sense of
meaning, purpose and clear cut character are not people who
play introspective power games . . . but people who have
taken a stand and are committed to a particular direction.

Consequently any leader must be overtly committed to a
course greater than him/herself and create an environment
where people within the organisation can also make a similar
commitment. A leader must also create a context where hope
is generated.

What we hope for and our expectations of the future are
the essence of our personalities. However, modern social
science has to an extent propogated the myth that what we
are today is determined by our past experiences.[11]

On the contrary, I believe that what we are now is determined not so much by our socialisation experiences, but by
what we hope to become and create in the future. The per-
severance of the Comrades runner is determined not so much
by the past, but by the hope of completing the challenge and
going the extra mile.

During therapy, the people I have seen improve dramati-
cally have all rediscovered a fundamental sense of meaning,
purpose and hope in their lives, which pulls them forward.
During counselling I prefer to work in the here-and-now and

future, rather than toward 'insight' generated from the past — because insight alone does not generate change.

The 'psychopathology' of the average citizen stems, I believe, in large part from having *unrealistic* expectations (of marriage, relationships in general and a search for happiness through material wealth) or having *no* expectations of the future. The pain and loss generated from a broken relationship or retrenchment means coming to terms with a 'lost future' and recreating a different one that offers a sense of hope and a meaning to life.

The greatness of the Hebrew Bible, says Campolo, illustrates the necessity of hope, pointing out that 'when the old men no longer dream dreams, and the young people have lost their vision — the people shall perish'.

Consequently, a fundamental task of any leader is to create a context where hope is created for a better future, that instils a sense of commitment and purpose in people.

COMPETENCIES OF VISION

At the end of the day, while it is important to know why vision is an essential component of leadership, what specifically do excellent leaders do to actualise this in their organisations?

The results of the leadership research reveal five core competencies that distinguished excellent from average leadership in managing attention through vision. The words in brackets refer to the essential focus of each activity.

❑ Develops and communicates a clear vision of the future of the organisation or department in order to provide direction for people. (Future vision)

❑ Expects uncompromising standards of excellence and concern with improving previous standards in pursuit of objectives. (Excellence)

❏ Creates focus and transmits clarity concerning what is expected from employees. (Focus on fundamentals)

❏ Expresses a sense of mission that catches people's attention, inspires commitment and transforms purpose into action. (Attention)

❏ Seeks to understand what is preventing an organisation or department from growing and achieving its objectives. (Current reality)

The followers of excellent leaders rated their superiors significantly higher on all five competencies (with a mean score of 35,5 out of 45) compared to the followers of average leaders (22,8). It is important however to remember that there is still room for improvement amongst the excellent group.

✦

CHAPTER VI

CREATING MEANING THROUGH COMMUNICATION

INTRODUCTION

This refers to both the ability to communicate a vision *and* the ability to provide meaning for people in the organisation.

All organisations depend on the existence of shared meanings and interpretations of reality which facilitate co-ordinated action. Indeed, my research found that the greater the perceptual overlap between the leader and his/her followers, the better the leader.

This shared meaning needs to be skilfully communicated and involves more than verbal expression.

Leaders are constantly looking for innovative ways of conveying a message, using symbols and graphic ideas in order to create an emotional richness to their message. The purpose of this communication is to influence and organise meaning for members of the organisation so that they feel empowered as they act in concert to create synergy and alignment in activity. Without meaning that guides action, dispersement and fragmentation will be the order of the day.

Warren Bennis found that many of his interviewees were not especially articulate in the conventional sense but displayed the ability to create the right metaphor. For example 'one man I interviewed had a safety belt on his chair of the type found on aeroplanes ... His purpose: to communicate to his staff that the enterprise is taking off.'[1]

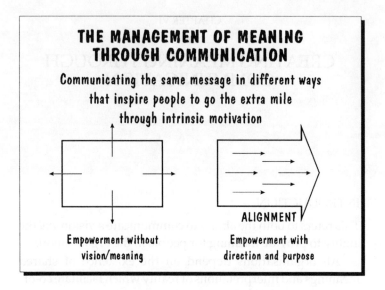

THE MANAGEMENT OF MEANING
THROUGH COMMUNICATION

Communicating the same message in different ways
that inspire people to go the extra mile
through intrinsic motivation

ALIGNMENT

Empowerment without   Empowerment with
vision/meaning   direction and purpose

HEALING OUR LAND: TWO-WAY COMMUNICATION

A vision that is not skilfully communicated throughout the organisation is like a car, pointing in the right direction, without keys and a driver — useless. A vision, or for that matter any idea, requires an understanding and acceptance before people are energised to action. This means that the leader has to *create* an audience who is willing to pay attention to the vision. It is easy to blame people as lazy and ignorant. The leadership challenge, however, requires accepting *responsibility* to get the message across in a way that people can understand and relate to.

Communication is a two way process. Indeed, a major problem under the apartheid regime was talking *at* people, while their responses often fell on deaf ears and were ignored. If people are expected to listen to the leader, the leader needs to *earn* this willingness to listen.

Neal Chapman from Southern Life points out in a UCT Business school videotape that 'The polarisation of communities in South Africa has been so marked that we have tended to live in our own compartments. Consequently we need to go out to different communities and understand other people's worlds.'[2] Indeed, it is the willingness to listen and hear people, to get close to our customers at work and in the market place, that lies at the heart of communication.

Although this is nothing more than common sense, if we are to stay in business, two way communication requires a fundamental shift of mind on the part of leaders. Leaders must be accountable for their actions and move from the expectation of being served as the 'lord of the manor' to serving others and enabling them to perform.

The days of issuing edicts are as dead as the kwagga. The massive reaction of Eastern Europe and the demise of apartheid in South Africa bears testimony to the folly of exclusive top-down autocratic style of communication. Establishing a 'user friendly' two-way communication environment is then simply a pragmatic way of responding more effectively to evolving consumer demands.

The leader also has an important role to communicate the changes in the business environment and the way in which these may impact on the organisation, and consequently which strategies that are adopted in this regard.[3] (See Chapter II)

CONSCIOUSLY COMMUNICATING CULTURE

'The manager of the future needs to be flexible, tolerant and develop superb communication skills in a new South Africa.'[4]
John Hall — CEO Barlow Rand

A vision or idea requires an acceptance of that idea which involves *creating an 'audience'* willing to pay attention to the vision. The best ideas are only as good as their ability to attract attention in the social environment. Leadership creates a *'new audience'* for its ideas because it alters the shape of understanding by transmitting information in such a way that it fixes and secures traditions. Leadership, by communicating meaning, creates a *commonwealth of learning* and that in turn is what effective organisations are. In this manner the leader becomes a social architect who understands the organisation and shapes the way it works. Social architecture is intangible although it governs the way people act and the values, norms and contents and quality of inter-personal interaction. In this way employees align themselves behind a vision, and become committed to it as their behaviour and thinking is reinforced on a daily basis.

Change in the social architecture or culture of an organisation requires attention to it's structure, policies, procedures, reward systems and hidden, often implicit assumptions about the way things are done — all of which reinforce the company's vision. If an organisation is to be transformed the leader must create and articulate new values and norms, offer new visions, and use a variety of tools to transform, support and institutionalise new meanings and directions.

Edgar Schein points out the interdependence between leadership and organisational culture. Leadership influences and is influenced by the organisation's myths, rules, folk lores, values, policies, attitudes and behaviour which are both implicit and explicit.[5]

In this regard Bobby Godsell points out that in order to accomodate people of different cultures into managerial positions in future, we need to make our own expectations and culture explicit.[6] The onus is on South African leaders to develop superb communication skills in order to accomodate the rich diversity of cultures into organisations in a manner that allows the human and organisational potential to be realised. This doesn't mean adopting a 'fit in or leave' mentality which indicates a regressive or stability-orientation in a changing environment. Rather, leaders need to learn to com-

municate in ways that transcend differences and create alignment, while simultaneously encouraging the human diversity that is vital for growth and change.

INTRINSIC MOTIVATION AND MEANING

'Managerial work is undergoing such enormous and rapid change that
managers are reinventing their profession as they go. Managers have
little precedent to guide them, as they are faced with extraordinary levels
of complexity and inter-dependency and eroding sources of traditional
power and ineffectiveness of old motivational tools. In short leadership
is more difficult, yet more critical than ever.'[7]

One of the critical success factors identified by CEO's is the
ability to motivate people and to deal with interpersonal
issues.[8] Indeed the critical question constantly asked by managers during consultation and training is: How do I motivate
my people? How can I get them to be more productive? How
can I meet people's expectations for improved quality of life
and job satisfaction?

In response traditional management training has pointed
to using the 'big stick' or 'variety of carrots' to motivate
people. There is no doubt that fear works in the short term,
but eventually leads to *avoidance* behaviour. Rewards work
perhaps a little more effectively, but their constant allocation
and distribution is exhausting for the manager. Herzberg has
also shown that money is not a motivating factor, but a
maintenance factor, where if people believed that they are
getting a fair wage, they will *not be dissatisfied*.[9]

The problem with these motivators is that they are extrin-
sic and dependent on the manipulation and enforcement of
the manager. They are also based on the Freudian assumption
that all people seek pleasure and/or the avoidance of pain.
However, ultimately people will only go the extra mile to
perform if they have a sense of intrinsic meaning or purpose
in what they and their organisation are trying to accomplish.

From a human behavioural perspective there are essentially three approaches to understand motivation.

1. *The will to pleasure* (Freud)

   Essentially people are motivated by sexual and aggressive drives.

2. *The will to power* (Adler)

   People are motivated by a desire to gain power over someone or something else.

3. *The will to meaning* (Frankl)

   The fundamental motivational force is the desire to find life *(personal and organisational)* meaningful.

Clearly a case can be made in a world that demands 'instant gratification' and 'fast foods' and constantly uses sexual connotations in advertising — that pleasure is a driving force behind human behaviour.

One look at the power plays and backstabbing in politics and business would be equally convincing to assert that people are driven to gain power over someone or something else.

However, Victor Frankl points out that the 'will to pleasure' and the 'will to power' are distorted, self destructive searches for the 'will to meaning'. Fundamentally, the primary motivational force in people is to find life meaningful — to have a fundamental purpose in your life and work for which you alone have been created.

Frankl comments on the consequence and the shallowness of the instant gratification ethic, and of the search for pleasure and power:

> 'A characteristic of this present age is the increasing freedom of people from traditional ties and associated systems of mores, folk-ways and religious disciplines, coupled with the fact that instead of flowering in their new found freedom, a large share have become muddled, confused, highly anxious and self driving, and in general resort to ways of escaping their freedom.

'Such modern maladies as alcoholism, increased divorce rates, overuse and experimental use of drugs and the general entertainment and recreation manias have been linked with this desperate flight or search.'[10]

The unheard cry for meaning is the mass neurosis of today and perhaps the most untapped human resource organisations have at their disposal. Frankl cites the example of the Director of the Behavioural Therapy centre in New York who states that many of the people in therapy had good jobs and 'successful' careers but wanted to kill themselves because they found life meaningless.

Understanding the fundamental human need to seek meaning helps to explain the frustration people feel when they are underutilised: 'Most of us are looking for a calling, not a job. Most of us, like the assembly line worker, have jobs that are too small for our spirits — jobs that are not big enough for people.'[11]

The fundamental premise underpinning many managerial theories concerning motivation needs to be challenged. The behaviouristic approach sees people as beings whose behaviour is totally determined by inner drives and outer conditions and consequently favours objectivity and causal explanations. The Freudian psychoanalytic approach, in turn, views homo-sapiens as reactive animals controlled and unable to escape the id's influence.

A problem arises in that these approaches are based on a reductionistic view of people as being controlled by inner drives and external circumstances (with no choice) and consequently are unable to cope with the need to develop new products and services that are the lifeblood of the growing organisation. While there is no doubt that a vast majority of the workforce are 'conditioned responders', this is as much due to a leaderless, demotivating work environment that has produced the 'push button' mentality where 'I, the manager,

think and you act' — rather than the inherent nature of people
to do mindless work.

The other problem with these reductionistic approaches is
that they evoke the self fulfilling prophecy of incompetence.
The manager in turn gets a payoff from blaming incompetent
workers, his control is reinforced and he goes away with his
world view confirmed — 'I'm good, you're bad'. Most training programmes do not address this mindset as they in turn
produce their own conditioned responders or dinosaurs of
the information age.

In contrast, business survival needs to develop what
Robert Carkhuff calls 'processors of information'. These processors elicit and expand their information inputs and sources, processing them by factoring in the significant
contributions, and then dedicating this processing toward
incrementally greater productivity. They enjoy the creative
negotiations of their own values and with the requirements
of the information age, and are increasingly synergistic as
they move toward their personal mission.[12]

A processor of information, in contrast to the mechanistic
mentality of conditioned responders, has a fundamental purpose that pulls him/her forward and guides his/her behaviour. The behaviouristic and Freudian approaches to people
have no answer for the intrinsically directed person.

ACTUALISING MEANING AT WORK

How then can the leader create a work context that is
meaningful and produce processors of information who are
self motivated? How can managers tap the same inner drive
and concentration of workers who in their spare time become
a team of footballers who spend hours voluntarily kicking a
ball around? How can the work environment generate a
similar commitment of 11 000 people who choose to spend
eleven hours on the road every year on 31 May, running

90 km? I doubt indeed whether these people are driven primarily by pleasure or for power motives. I certainly don't find the last part of a canoe marathon or a triathlon pleasurable, but nevertheless find the experience deeply meaningful and creative. What will it take to channel the same kind of effort into work?

Frankl suggests three ways in which life can be made meaningful:

Firstly, a person can find meaning in what he/she gives to life in terms of *creative activities and values*. Secondly, a person can get meaning by means of what he/she takes from life, that is by means of *personal experiences*. Thirdly, a person can find meaning in taking a particular attitude towards an event which *cannot be changed*.[13]

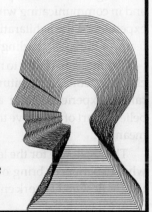

ACTUALISATION OF MEANING

● Creative Values
An outlet for self-expression
and creativity

● Experiential Values
Uplifting, motivating
experiences at home or work

● Attitudinal Values
Choice, toward circumstances
you can't change

1. Creative values

These are values which create or produce something. People spend their lives looking for creative ways to express themselves. The creative urge starts in childhood games, extends to the sportsfield and cultural pursuits at school and spearheads the choice of career. The home executive needs fulfilment in creating her home although often her creative urges are lived out through her children.

At work, creative outlets range from construction and architecture, to creatively designing computer programmes and choosing and enacting a particular business strategy. There are any number of creative ways of interacting and motivating people. One can even avoid the boss creatively, and 'commit fraud' as many perplexed employers will testify.

The challenge then for any leader is to find out what people hope to create at work, to channel this into organisationally effective behaviour and then finally to design an environment where the creative juices flow, thus unleashing human potential.

2. Experiential values

Meaning comes from experiencing the creative work of others and in communicating with the beauty of nature. We have all experienced the exhilaration of being part of a truly creative team, or the spine tingling shivers evoked by beautiful music.

The desire to return to nature, reflected in the trend toward choosing cottage furniture, thatch houses, executive river rafting experiences and a lifestyle out of the rat race is, I believe, part of the move to seek experiential values — to find meaning.

The challenge for the leader in organisations is to identify what experiences bring out the best in people at work, and then to design the work environment in a way that maximises these experiences.

3. Attitudinal Values

Attitudinal values are vital in those areas of limiting factors confronting us daily at work or home. Limiting factors refer to circumstances that we are powerless to change — retrenchments, conflict at work, failure in one form or another. We cannot change what happens to us, but we can choose how we respond to these crises.

Since suffering is unavoidable, and part of being human, it seems much wiser to adopt a philosophy of life which accepts a certain amount of suffering or even gives it a positive value. Life is not anything, it is only an opportunity of something. Further than this, always remember, it is not the load that breaks us down, but the way we carry it.

Everyone, at one time or another, experiences adversity at work. We are given a choice concerning how we respond to conflict, failure and even retrenchment. How can these situations be reframed and used to your advantage?

Conflict, for instance, can be viewed as an opportunity to resolve disagreements. The opposite to love is not hate, but apathy. Consequently a couple who fight are very much involved with and in need of each other. It is from this basis of need that understanding, rather than defensive behaviour, can proceed.

The same choice of attitude applies to apparent failure. Thomas Edison was once asked how he felt when his experiments 'had failed' 9 999 times. Astonished, he replied that these weren't failures, but an opportunity to learn to do something differently. And the 10 000th time he 'saw the light'.

Every leader has a vital role to play in reframing failure as 'feedback' and an opportunity to learn something. Just as the glass of water can be half full or half empty, leaders need to see opportunities as challenges rather than threats. If life gives you a lemon, then make lemonade! If leaders don't develop this ability to reframe problems as challenges — and to communicate this optimism — their followers can be excused for wanting to leave the organisation. Leaders *must create* the social architecture of an organisation in a way that taps into people's needs for intrinsic motivation and provides a context where creative, experiential and attitudinal values converge with those of the organisation.

SOUTH AFRICAN LEADERS

Gail Kelly's research found that Chief Executive Officers had superb communication skills both on interpersonal and organisational levels. The importance of being available and visible to promote two-way communication is underscored below:

> 'I make myself available to my executives immediately *for business and private needs.'* (Executive number 21)

> 'My days are totally unstructured — they involve a few meetings and appointments and a lot of walking about and chatting to people at all levels. I believe in heavy networking.' (Executive number 22)

> 'I spend the greatest portion of my day moving around and talking to people, we are a great company for visible management.'[14]

In terms of the critical difference between average and excellent leaders, the following five competencies emerged from my leadership research:

❏ Conscious communication of a focus that is meaningful for people, through verbal expression, symbols and graphic expression of ideas (communicating creative values).

❏ The fostering of strategic change while maintaining a clear purpose for the organisation (meaning in change).

❏ The communication through understanding and empathy of a sense of meaningfulness in work (communication).

❑ A raising of aspirations, shaping of values and mobilisation of potential of followers in a way that improves the quality of their lives (creating meaning).

❑ The inducing of followers to act for common goals, thereby creating synergy and alignment in action (synergy through meaning).

In summary John Hall from Barlow Rand offers the following advice for aspirant leaders:

'Don't rush in (for the sake of making an impact). Get to know people and practice a touch of humility. Remember what motivated you is probably what motivates other people. You are a human being . . . try not to forget that.'[15]

CHAPTER VII

TRUST

INTRODUCTION

The following examples, involving South African leaders elaborating on the importance of trust, were taken from the recent 'Developing a Philosophy of Management' videotape produced by the University of Cape Town's Business school.

Peter Searle points out the fundamental importance of a leader who supports people and relies on them for results.[1] This presupposes trusting people to deliver the goods, based on high but realistic expectations, and on the leader being available in a non-intrusive way if needed.

This necessitates the realisation, says Vic Hammond of Edgars, that other people have their own ways of doing things (and expressing themselves creatively) that might be different and better than your way.[2]

Trust is a two-way process that has to be *earned* by both the leaders and followers, and is vital in allowing potential to develop. Ian McCrae, for example, believes that a critical ingredient in his own leadership ability was 'support from my superior who expressed confidence in me and space to fulfil my responsibilities.'[3]

Trust is about consistency, reliability and predictability. It is about being congruent in word and deed and about fairness in dealing with people. It is an unspoken bond: 'The trust between me and my executive team is such that no notes are needed. If I say yes then they know I mean yes, and that I will remember that I said yes, and that if it turns sour, I'll take the rap with them.'[4]

On an interpersonal level too, Grant Thomas of Malbak, underscores the importance of trust and consistency as a basis for any communication.:

'Be consistent in your dealings with people. People respond best when they know where they are. Consistency is the key to handling people.'[5]

It cannot be overemphasised that trust is the basis for any successful human activity that leaves both parties satisfied and opens the door to future relationships. However, it goes against the grain of office politics and is at a premium when we constantly hear stories of deceit, lying, self interest and cover ups which are the preferred ways of leaders who have stood on foundations of clay.

FOLLOWER EXPECTATIONS OF LEADERS

Fundamental to trust is the understanding and meeting of follower expectations. Leaders, by definition, can only lead if they have followers. Leadership can only deliver and get things done through other people. Committed voluntary followers are a leader's hands, legs and eyes in the case of keeping the leader informed.

Because any leader is dependent on people, it is not what the leader himself does or thinks that is important, but how others experience and interpret this leadership behaviour that will determine the action that they take. This illustrates the reciprocal nature of the leader-follower relationship and the ongoing cycle of influence of both parties. The only way that the relationship can be complementary to both parties is if it is built on a foundation of trust.

Each contact between leader and follower is a 'moment of truth' or opportunity for leaders to be congruent in word and deed. Consequently interpersonal skills are vital and leaders need to be constantly aware of the impact that they are having on others.

Kouzes and Posner, however, point out in research involving over 5 000 followers that the primary reason leaders lose their credibility is because of insensitivity to constituents. This includes a failure to empathise and understand people's perspectives either through arrogance, pride, failure to listen or by taking people for granted.[6] The leader operating from this egocentric perspective expects people to serve him/her rather than serving others.

Power in service of self must inevitably evoke conflict resulting in a win/lose situation. In contrast, transformational leadership relies on socialised power in service of others and engenders commitment rather than compliance.

Leaders also lose credibility through lying. Kouzes and Posner cite a recent New York Times survey where only 32 % of the public believes that most corporate executives are honest. Clearly this indicates a difference between what people expect and what they think they are receiving in terms of credible leadership.

Credibility and empathy can only be earned by being in touch with people. It is not enough to say that you understand the concerns, needs and aspirations of your people — this has to be *demonstrated*. The Oxford Dictionary word for leadership means 'to go, to travel, to guide'. Management, on the other hand, originates from the Latin word 'manus' (hand) — to handle things. You can manage from a seated position, but leadership involves using your feet (and head) and travelling to your people. The journey of trust begins with spending a good deal of time at the coal-face and any leader who doesn't want to embark on this human journey cannot claim to have credibility.

COMMITMENT STARTS WITH YOU

The successful leader has to pay attention to building trust on an organisational and individual level. I will initially deal with the former.

Trust is the 'lubrication' which makes it possible for organisations to work, and it is the determined persistent stance of the leader, more than anyone else, that creates this trust. Trust is gained by doing the right thing with absolute clarity and reliability. Put away the hidden agendas — take a stand and stay the course even if this means sailing against the wind. Maintaining and communicating basic goals and values against the odds is as important as selecting the right vision and strategies in the first place.

Warren Bennis and Burt Nanus see trust as the 'glue that maintains an organisation's integrity', and implies accountability, predictability and reliability and is established by the clear articulation of the organisation's position by leaders consistently advocating a course of action.

The most common statement made about Bennis' 90 leaders by their board members and staff was that they were 'all of a piece' and congruent in word, vision and deed. In this way leaders enrol themselves (and others) in the belief of their ideals and visions, and their behaviour exemplifies the ideals in action. Outstanding leaders place a premium on reliability, persistence and clarity of a position which they continually advocate.[7] I am constantly reminded of the commitment of exceptional people such as Mahatma Gandhi, Martin Luther King and Mother Theresa, who have made enormous sacrifices, sometimes even facing death for causes in which they believed, because they chose an angle and stuck resolutely to it.

While corporate survival is often a matter of life and death, the leader has to be overtly committed before he/she can expect the commitment of the troops. Martin Luther King captures the commitment underpinning trust in a nutshell, by stating that 'A person who won't die for something is not fit to live'.

Commitment requires courage to adopt a view that refuses to be ambiguous and may stand out sharply and clearly from prevailing opinion. Change, by its very nature involves confronting the unknown and confronting fear. However, 'Courage faces fear and thereby masters it. Cowardice represses fear and is therefore mastered by it. Courageous men never lose the zest for living even though their life situation is zestless. Cowardly men, overwhelmed by the uncertainties of life, lose the will to live. We must constantly build dykes of courage to hold back the flood of fear.'[8]

Leadership is not about winning popularity contests, but persistent rational dedication which *offers people a choice* — either you're also committed, or you get left behind. Better the devil you know than the devil you don't.

Ultimately it is the leader's relentless dedication to an idea, or mission of the organisation *as well* as his/her commitment to people that engages trust.

The significance of 'staying the course' or consistency is particularly relevant in the calculated risk-taking component of leadership. Innovation — any new idea — by definition will not be accepted at first. Innovation causes resistance and opposition to form. It takes repeated attempts, endless demonstrations, and monotonous rehearsals before innovation can be accepted and internalised by any organisation. It requires courageous patience.

INTERPERSONAL SKILLS — THE VEHICLE FOR TRUST BUILDING

A leader's eyes, feet, hands and heart are dependent on the people he/she works with. *People* translate vision into reality or strategic planning into action. Consequently every successful leader must master key interpersonal skills that maximise the quality of one-to-one relationships.

Any person's ability to be happy is directly dependent on their ability to establish and maintain productive interpersonal relationships that fulfil our fundamental human need for acceptance and belonging. Unbelievably, however, these key skills are seldom if ever taught at school or in tertiary education — which tends to concentrate exclusively on technical skills. Indeed, Robert Carkhuff contends that more people have lost their jobs due to a lack of human/people skills than their lack of technical skills necessary to do those jobs.[9]

Carkhuff in his 'productivity enhancing process' points out the primary importance of attending, responding, personalising and initiating skills as a vehicle to *demonstrate* understanding and to empower people to take responsibility for their own lives. These skills are the basis from which to express empathy and to develop '*trust*' — which is the basis of any healthy relationship.

The first stage of any relationship is *involvement*. Leaders, says Carkhuff, need to consciously understand and practice attending skills, such as body language, observation and listening, in order to demonstrate care and concern (verbally and non-verbally) and to involve people with us.[9] This includes understanding the dynamics underpinning individual change and defensive behaviour, as well as the ability to read 'body language' which together with 'tone of voice' is far more important to communication than the verbal message.

Once involvement has been earned, the leader must respond in a way that demonstrates an understanding of other people's 'frame of reference'. Empathy is the ability to put yourself in someone else's shoes and to *demonstrate* this understanding in a non-judgemental fashion. Only when people have been heard can trust develop.

Consequently, commitment and participation are dependent on the conscious application of attending, listening and responding skills in preference to the traditional 'threshold of deafness' that is the norm of the hierarchical leader.

As previously mentioned, congruence in word and deed is vital to establishing trust. Any underlying attitude that does not recognise human dignity and competence will be picked up in the leader's body language and will foster cynicism and mistrust. It is impossible not to communicate — even silence or inaction is communicating something.

This may sound as if every leader should also be a psychologist in order to be effective! In essence, however, the message is simple. Leadership is a human 'business' and consequently an understanding of people and interpersonal skills are vital to expressing all the competencies of leadership and motivating followers to go the extra mile.

SUMMARY

Research involving recognised South African business leaders who have earned trust, points out the importance of being in touch with people, having superb interpersonal skills, exhibiting candour and putting people in a position to achieve their goals.[10] This requires autonomous, delegated authority which empowers people and openly shared goals and values that allow collaborative individualism.[11] In this way people experience ownership as the leader relies on people and their strengths. Trust is dependent on people's contributions being recognised and their accomplishments celebrated, and implies that the leader has *human* and *situational empathy*.

Through a combination of interpersonal trust, and the leader consistently and rationally advocating a position, people become 'enrolled' and committed to a vision that has

meaning for them. In essence then, trust is developed through
the exhibition of the following five competencies.[12]

5 COMPETENCIES

- Congruent in word and deed.
- Expresses positive regard and belief in others (trust).
- Expresses accountability, predictability and reliability of an organisation's position.
- Articulates and embodies a moral code that cares about people (innate worth of people).
- Relies on people and enables them to control and enrich their lives.

CHAPTER VIII

✦

THE MANAGEMENT AND DEPLOYMENT OF SELF

INTRODUCTION

John Hall, when asked what he gave up when he became a senior manager, replied:

'I missed the instant gratification of doing deals — I also learnt that loneliness goes with responsibility.[1]'

The further up you go in the organisation, the more the leader needs to be able to manage him/herself because — 'the buck stops here'. Neal Chapman illustrates the increasing importance of self management and realistic expectations that go with the territory:

'The further up you go, the greater and more complex the decisions you have to make. You will never get perfect data or unbiased recommendations. Take the decisions and don't brood on them. If you achieve a fifty percent correctness you are doing exceedingly well.[2]'

At the end of the day the personality, character and energy of the leader is a critical factor behind organisational success. However the stress that goes with the territory is also enormous. This stress can either be used negatively (distress) or positively (eustress) in terms of the intrapersonal impact on the leader *and* those people around him/her (interpersonal) — depending on how the leader manages him/herself.

Top executives spend approximately ninety percent of their time with others and much of this time is taken up by people's problems.[3] Consequently, without competent self management skills, leaders will do more harm than good.

85

The term iatrogenic refers to illness caused by doctors and hospitals as side effects of medical intervention. Experience in counselling people has shown me too that the therapist can never have a neutral impact on the patient — they either get better, or worse. Likewise, the leader can be, and often is, a stress carrier, causing rather than curing problems. The message then is straightforward — you can't manage others until you can manage yourself.

Endless organisational development literature and bitter personal experience is unequivocal — if there is a problem in the organisation it is invariably at the top. Vaughn Beals of Harley Davidson describes vividly how the company tried every form of 'fix-it' consultant and culture routine until they had exhausted every possibility but one. The problem, Beals found, lay with himself.[4]

The management of self starts with *personalising* responsibility for the negative impact you are having on others and your own self destructive behaviour, and committimg yourself to change. Until the blaming attitude of 'change them, not me' alters in every relationship, from the home to the sports field and lofty heights of corporate life — no growth is possible. The following Taoist story from ancient China illustrates the eternal wisdom of assuming personal responsibility for change:

> 'When Yen Ho was about to take up his duties as tutor to the heir of Ling, Duke of Wei, he went to Ch'u Po Yu for advice. 'I have to deal,' he said, 'with a man of depraved and murderous disposition . . . How is one to deal with a man of this sort?'
>
> 'I am glad that you asked this question . . . The first thing you must do is not to improve him, but to improve yourself.'[5]

EMOTIONAL WISDOM

Wisdom unfortunately often comes from the knocks of life, gleaned from personal suffering and learning the hard way — by making mistakes. Seldom can 'it' be taught because there is a profound difference between hearing something intellectually and owning 'the truth' emotionally and spiritually. Indeed, principles of psychotherapy and adult education constantly refer to the importance of allowing people to discover things for themselves.

There is also no guarantee that we will learn from experience. Homo-sapiens have a remarkable ability to construct elaborate defence mechanisms, such as denial, rationalisation and blaming others — all of which externalise responsibility for change.

While psychological defences are adaptive and indeed necessary to cope short term, their rigid, consistent employment over an extended period simply means that we stagnate, feel trapped, and become victims of circumstances beyond our control. Consequently, thirty years experience is simply reliving the same experiences thirty times.

What then are the competencies that constitute the creative deployment of self and emotional wisdom?

Fundamentally, learning proceeds from having:

❑ Knowledge of one's strengths and weaknesses.
❑ Ability to discern gaps between one's strengths and weaknesses and the organisation's needs.
❑ Capacity to develop and nurture these with discipline.

People who have developed a sense of personal mastery have a positive self regard or high but realistic self concept and are consequently not afraid to admit weaknesses. Their orientation is one of growth and continual improvement — of self actualisation. Consequently, negative feedback is not seen as criticism but 'an opportunity to grow'. The result of positive self regard is to induce the same in other people, indicating the influence of the leader's presence and a tendency to expect from others what you expect of yourself. Consequently, what is fundamental to individual and organisational growth, is the leader's view of him/herself, and the view of others, as being either creative or incompetent.

Bennis and Nanus, in their study of ninety leaders from all spectrums of society, found that positive self regard was related to emotional wisdom, which included five key skills:

❑ The ability to accept people as they are and to use empathy to understand people's worlds.

❑ The ability to approach relationships and problems in terms of the present, rather than the past.

❑ The ability to treat those who are close to you with the same courteous attention that you extend to strangers and casual acquaintances.

❑ The ability to trust others.

❑ The ability to get on without constant approval and recognition from others.[6]

SOUTH AFRICAN LEADERS — MASTERS OF SELF

Bennis and Nanus and Kelly discovered that leaders had an interesting cognitive approach when responding to failure. Leaders simply did not think about failure nor did they use synonymous words for the concept. Instead, they saw failure as feedback from which they learnt to do something differently. This, in turn, assumes responsibility to initiate and sustain change or an internal locus of control.[7]

Leaders constantly face criticism and the consequent need to understand events as they really are. This willingness to face current reality is used, together with a vision of the future, to create dynamic tension and to move toward actualising an appropriate strategy for the organisation.[8]

The following authors elaborate on the management of self (see Table IV:I). Boyatsis found the following competencies to include effective self-management — accurate self assessment, self control, stamina, concern with impact and self confidence.[9] Limmerick found that effective Australian C.E.O.'s were pro-active, individualistic and self aware, exhibited change management skills, were good at motivating and had a sense of personal mastery.[10] Senge defines personal mastery as the ability to accept responsibility for change and the achievement of a clear vision. This presupposes that leaders identify and challenge their own belief systems or 'mental models' that hinder the sense of creative deployment of self.[11]

Tom Peters points to the importance of self esteem and continuous learning to expand 'self',[12] while Kelly concurs that these leadership competencies *can* be developed. South African leaders, she found, were continually looking for new challenges, were prepared to risk, loved work, were alert to learn and had confidence and faith in their own judgement.[13] Ball and Asbury point out that leadership requires energy, initiative and time at the 'coal-face'[14] as the leader becomes a role model for others.[15] This requires the ability to foster change through understanding human nature, 'tolerating ambiguity and accepting responsibility'.[16] In addition, the leader requires mastery of core thinking, planning and relating skills.[17]

In terms of the above, five competence statements were constructed describing the ability of South African leaders to manage themselves. In my research, both sets of leaders rated themselves highly on each statement with an overall mean of 34,7 out of 45 for the excellent sample, compared to the self rating of 34,8 amongst the average leaders.

However, the follower ratings show a statistically significant difference. Followers of excellent leaders rated them on a mean of 35,8 compared to 23,3 for the average leaders by their followers. Consequently, leader self-evaluation alone is not a good indicator of leadership competence. Any meaningful assessment must take into account *follower perceptions and experiences of leadership.*

The five competencies relating to self management which distinguish excellent leadership include:

❑ Development of personal strengths and weaknesses by the leader, through self awareness and a realistic view of him/herself (self awareness).

❑ Commitment to self development and continual learning (growth and change).

❑ Perception of change and threatening situations as a challenge and opportunity for growth (cognitive hardiness).

❑ Acceptance of responsibility for creating individual life experience rather than blaming situations or people for misfortune (responsibility and internal locus of control).

❑ Ability to diagnose and change inappropriate behaviour and independently to take constructive action (personal mastery).

There remains, however, a question concerning why there is significantly greater perceptual overlap amongst the excellent leaders/followers, while the gap between the average sample is so much greater. The reasons for the average leader's 'blindness' will be dealt with in Chapter 10.

✦
EMPOWERMENT

INTRODUCTION

Chapter II looked at the changing human environment that confronts leaders and the imperative to create a context where people are willing, able and allowed to perform. This is important in two respects. Firstly in order to retain the best people in your organisation, who will leave if they don't find an environment that fosters personal growth and allows quality of life to be realised.

Secondly, leaders must empower people, because it is the quality of an organisation's human resources that determines in large part its competitive advantage. It is also the primary method by which leaders can impact on the burgeoning skills shortage that confronts business.

And so leaders have little choice but to understand and apply the crucial leadership competence of empowerment. Chapter II has looked at the problems faced by organisations, particularly the attitudes of its managers in 'growing people'. Unless these self defeating attitudes are dealt with, no growth can take place.

This chapter, however, aims at demystifying the nebulous concept of empowerment and offering specific guidelines that leaders can implement in their organisations. To do this, I will look at results from South African research and draw on examples of South African business leaders and their views on empowerment.

POWER — WIN/LOSE OR EXPANDABLE PIE?

Empowerment is often glibly bandied about in fashionable speeches and annual reports by the very people who hinder the growth and development of an organisation's human resources. This lip service arises because leaders do not understand what empowerment means, nor what changes they need to make in their own attitudes and behaviour before the effective development of people can occur.

Jay Hall points out that over eighty percent of managers operate from a premise that people are *incompetent*.[1] This is the underlying premise behind the rigid grading and administrative systems, performance appraisals, job descriptions and status symbols that characterise the hierarchical organisation. Managers holding this belief, operate from a win-lose power orientation where people are seen as pawns in the corporate game. This is precisely the way the average leaders in the South African study viewed their people.

Alternatively, leaders who view people as creative and competent operate from an expandable pie concept of power. The giving of power to get power leads to greater reciprocity of influence as the leader and follower are willing to be mutually influenced by one another.

Leadership from a transformational perspective sees everyone as a potential leader with the focus being to enable others to act through fostering collaboration and strengthening others. This involves competencies such as the effective use of power, developing others and the ability to cope with and initiate change from both the leader and follower. The leader then becomes a catalyst for growth, through attention to structured development opportunities for followers and in the expectations and manner in which he/she interacts with people.

Empowerment is an investment in your own and other people's future. Kouzes and Posner quote studies — when the leader shares power with other people, those people in turn feel more strongly attached to the leader and more committed to carrying out their duties and responsibilities effectively — they feel that a failure to carry out tasks lets themselves down, as well as the boss.

> 'When you strengthen others, your level of influence with them is increased. When you go out of your way on behalf of others — you build up credit with them. By strengthening others, you place yourself on the subordinates' side.'[2]

Clearly then, an axiom behind the effective development of subordinates is the acceptance of the responsibility to develop and empower people by leaders within an organisation who have the capacity and authority to make a difference.

Any organisational intervention or attempt to develop leadership must address the existing attitudes to power and people — otherwise change will be cosmetic. How one goes about this will be discussed in the last chapter of the book.

Eugene van As of Sappi, reinforces the fundamental change that must take place: 'The skills middle managers will need in future will be the same, but their attitudes will have to change. We need to believe that people are all human and capable of doing the same job.'[3]

The South African leadership research identified five specific competencies that describe the exhibition of empowerment by excellent leaders in an organisational context:

❏ The creation of conditions where employees are willing, able and allowed to perform job related activities (socialised power).

❏ The removal of organisational obstacles hindering personal growth in other people (aware of organisational constraints).

❏ The helping of people to achieve more accurate, more inspiring and more empowering views of reality (current reality).

❑ The viewing of people as creative and competent (positive regard).

❑ The creation and encouragement of an opportunity for self development and continual learning in others (developmental role).

These five competencies distinguish excellent from average leaders, in the eyes of their followers.

WHAT DOES AN EMPOWERED PERSON LOOK LIKE?

Firstly we need to recognise how an unempowered or disempowered person behaves (for they are certainly more common). People who feel powerless, be they managers or subordinates, tend to hoard whatever shreds of power they have and consequently adopt petty and dictatorial management styles. Powerlessness creates organisational systems where political skills become essential and 'covering yourself' and 'passing the buck' become the preferred style for handling inter-departmental differences.[4]

A quick 'dip stick' to identify a disempowered person is a preference to externalise blame, seeing the cause of the problem as external to themselves (the boss, the dog, the wife, etc). Further, since empowerment is both a consequence and competence of leadership, it follows that an empowered person will exhibit the four competencies of leadership. As previously mentioned, these include capturing attention through vision, communicating meaning, trust and self management.

Consequently, a leader is empowered in his/her own right and empowers others in turn. An empowered person expresses elements of all the competence statements previously described, particularly those of:

❑ Nurturing and developing strengths and weaknesses, with a realistic view of oneself.

❑ Experiencing life as having a high degree of meaning and opportunity.
❑ Being committed to self development and continual learning.
❑ Having a clearly defined sense of responsibility for initiating change.
❑ Independently processing information and initiating action.

Tom Peters points out that an empowered person sees change as central to growth and as a leader, is able to create challenges for others out of the change process.[5] This necessitates an ability to think clearly and to tolerate ambiguity. The empowered person has a sense of personal mastery or a belief that he/she can initiate change to the benefit of self and the organisation.

This presupposes that the individual is willing, able and allowed to develop and take initiative, says Linda Human[6], and has the sensory awareness to diagnose ineffectual activity, and independently implement the necessary corrective actions according to a specific goal or vision. In this way people become processors and creators of new information and products, thereby generating organisational growth and renewal, rather than responding in a prescribed way to selected stimuli.

In essence, leadership involves *learning from and applying experience* (which will be dealt with in the next chapter, explaining in detail the reasons behind ineffective and effective leadership).

FROM THEORY TO PRACTICE

If recognised South African business leaders had not been empowered by their own leaders during their progress up the

corporate ladder, they would in all likelihood not have realised their potential.

Bobby Godsell talks about the support and regular guidance from a mentor who helped to sort out alternatives and
consequences of decisions that were not black and white, but
shades of grey.[7]

Jeff Liebesman concurs, on the importance of encouragement from staff, shareholders and his executive team when
he first took over as leader of F.S.I., as well as the fundamental
support from family and customers.[8]

Vic Hammond from Edgars, points out the importance of
relying on the competence of people and giving them confidence, through the message that you want them to make
mistakes in order to learn. He also believes that part of empowering others is to be comfortable with your own way of
doing things, while at the same time realising that other
people have their own styles that are equally effective and
which must be accomodated by the leader.[9]

Research into effective managerial competencies in South
Africa by Adrienne Lapinsky points out the importance of
effective feedback to subordinates, while at the same time
allowing individuals to take personal responsibility for making changes and testing their effectiveness. An example from
Lapinsky's research illustrates the process of empowerment.

'I took on her development and I encouraged her to develop her job. I
regraded the job and it came out as a far bigger job than the traditional
job. She is now an integral part of the business . . . I have started looking
at giving people additional responsibilities. I am growing their jobs
within international and local standards. The carrot I am offering them
is to develop within their jobs with clear standards of performance. The
benefit is obviously also to the business.'[10]

THE HERMAN MILLER STORY

Herman Miller Inc has been the primary innovator in the
furniture industry for sixty years. Named as one of the hun-

dred best companies to work for in the United States, Herman
Miller also ranked ninth in Fortune Magazine's 1989 survey
of the most admired corporations, nestled among household
names like Boeing and Pepsi Co. In management excellence,
the company was placed even higher, ranking sixth.[11]

$100 invested in Herman Miller stock in 1975 had grown
in value to $4 854 by 1989. They are the most productive
company in the furniture business and the most innovative.
What is their secret? In a nutshell — it is the leadership of Max
de Pree and his predecessors.

The secret lies in the fact that the leaders had the strength
to abandon themselves to the wild ideas of others. Not only
experts but also the 'ordinary employees' whose suggestions
saved them 12 million dollars in 1987–88.

One day a month, top management report to workers on
the company productivity and profits — the kind of disclosure that is usually punishable by death in most South African
firms. Why do the employees care? Because they are owners
of the company — both emotionally and financially.

In essence Herman Miller is a place with integrity or a
sense of one's obligations — starting with employees. 'The art
of leadership,' says President Max de Pree 'lies in liberating
people to do what is required of them in the most effective
and humane way possible.' Thus the leader is the servant of
his/her followers in that he/she removes all the obstacles that
prevent them from doing their jobs. In short, the true leader
enables his or her followers to realise their full potential and
develop their own spirit of self management.

To do this effectively, leaders must have thought through
their beliefs about human nature, the role of the organisation,
the measurement of performance and a host of other issues.
The true leader listens to the ideas, needs, aspirations and
wishes of followers and then within the context of his/her

own well-developed beliefs — responds to these in an appropriate fashion.

De Pree points out that leadership is an art — something to be learned over time — and has to do with the weaving of relationships. While it is in vogue to talk about the quality of product and service, what about the quality of relationships, communication and our promises to each other?

CULTURAL DIVERSITY AND EMPOWERMENT

The new buzzword in South African business is cultural diversity. I've yet to find anyone who can clearly define the concept or actualise it better than the Herman Miller story.

Leaders, De Pree writes, must endorse a concept of persons. This begins with an understanding of the diversity of people's gifts, talents and skills.

Understanding and accepting diversity enables us to see that each of us is needed. It also enables us to think about being abandoned to the strengths of others, and admitting that we cannot do everything.

The simple act of recognising diversity in corporate life helps us to connect the great variety of gifts that people bring into service of the organisation. Diversity allows each of us to contribute in a special way, to the corporate effort. Recognising diversity helps us to understand the need we have for opportunity, equity and identity in the workplace. Recognising diversity in organisations gives people a chance to meet the fundamental human needs to find meaning, fulfillment and purpose, which are not solely relegated to private life.

When we think about leaders and the variety of gifts people bring to corporations and institutions, we see that the art of leadership lies in polishing, liberating and enabling those gifts, concludes De Pree. The process of understanding and actualising diversity can only occur through *leadership* that grabs people's attention through *our* attractive vision of the future. Communicating an organisational purpose (that is meaningful) builds trust and enables people to realise their potential through creating an empowering environment.

A fundamental reason then behind a lack of diversity in organisations lies in the control orientation of leaders and their views of people as incompetent. Consequently, the critical leverage point for recognising and unleashing human potential is leadership that creates an empowering environment.

LEADERSHIP PRECEDES EQUAL OPPORTUNITY

We have seen previously that a critical leverage point in implementing equal opportunity is the conducive attitudes and teaching skills of 'white managers'. If they don't create an environment where people are willing, able and allowed to perform, and commit themselves to removing organisational obstacles to growth, then no meaningful advancement can occur.

Consequently, any bottom-up equity programme must simultaneously be complemented by a top-down leadership programme that creates an environment where people are free to utilise their skills. Any equity programme should also fundamentally aim at creating leaders in their own right. The problems of marginality and inferiority need to be replaced by the leadership competencies of an internal locus of control and the ability to manage oneself. This extensive process can only occur with complementary line manager expectations. The good news is that it is indeed possible to develop leadership competence in people who have a basic education (Standard 8) as my experience in the Chamber of Mines over the last 18 months has shown.[12]

The link between leadership and, in particular, a vision of the future and its empowering and enabling effect on disadvantaged children, is underscored in Benjamin Singer's work,

'The Future Focussed Role Image.'[13] Singer quotes research where low performing students had almost no sense of their own future. Their future was strictly short term and they believed the ability to shape it was in the hands of fate.

On the other hand, successful students had a much greater personal sense of control over their future. They thought in time horisons of 5–10 years ahead. Interestingly, I.Q. and family background were *not* the key indicators of success. Some of the most unsuccessful students had genius I.Q.'s and came from the best of families. The key differentiator was a profound and positive vision of their future.

So when we ask our children what they want to be when they grow up, never treat their answers as trivial. We listen to show our children that their dreams of the future are signifi-cant. Our interest in their dreams in turn builds their con-fidence and ability to shape their own future. A similar process by the organisational leader is vital to the implemen-tation of any equal opportunity programme.

EMPOWERMENT . . . TAKES TIME

Previously, we have seen that the critical determinant of a person's development on the job is their boss or leader. This offers either a superb opportunity or a headache for the leader to develop people toward peak performance or to create committed people who are intrinsically motivated.

However, the process of development is akin to the nur-turing of children — time consuming and requiring specific competencies on the part of the leader/parent. The harsh reality is that few people are immediately competent when they start a job and lack the self confidence and tenacity to learn on their own. Conversely, a few structured moments each day, applying the right kind of leadership, delivers immense rewards for both the leader and the follower. In fact, the process of development is probably the most rewarding and essential part of any leader's job — if applied correctly.

I have drawn on the work of Kenneth Blanchard to illustrate the **transactional** process of matching the right leadership style to a person's developmental level in order to create competent, committed people in the shortest space of time.[14] In this respect the leader must take responsibility to apply the skills of situational leadership *before* blaming followers for not performing. Certainly the rewards of development — having motivated independent people — are worth it.

Blanchard points out that the situational leader needs three skills — *flexibility* of leadership styles, *diagnosis* of follower development level and matching the appropriate leadership style, *contracting* with followers concerning goals and objectives and the *delivery* of the appropriate leadership style.

Flexibility involves learning to use 'different strokes for different folks' — or the right style at the right time. There are, according to Blanchard, four different leadership styles, starting with *directing*, followed by *coaching*, then *supporting* and lastly *delegating*.

Each style differs in the amount of direction and support the leader provides and the amount of involvement in decision making. Directive behaviour is defined as the extent to which the leader tells the follower what to do, and when, where and why to do it. Directive behaviour is one-way communication from the leader to the follower. As the leader moves from directing, to coaching, through supporting to delegating, he/she uses progressively less directing as the people they are trying to influence *learn* to direct themselves.

Supportive behaviour is defined as the extent to which you develop a (two way) personal relationship with your people. In essence this includes the extent to which you listen, support and praise your followers. As the leadership style moves from directing to coaching, the amount of supportive behaviour increases, and increases further as you move toward supporting. However, as people become progressively more competent and confident in a task, and consequently become inner directed, supporting behaviour declines and the task can be delegated.

As the leader moves through the process from directing through to delegation, the amount of involvement and responsibility that followers have for decision-making also increases. If this does not happen, frustration will inevitably occur and people will receive the message that they are incompetent.

Flexibility of leadership style is dependent on *diagnosing* the developmental level and needs of people with respect to specific tasks and responsibilities. Diagnosis allows the leader to use the correct leadership style in the correct situation. This prevents the problem of leaving those alone who need to be directed, and harassing people who are competent, when delegation should be applied.[14]

People's performance is dependent on two aspects that make up developmental level — their competence and commitment. Competence has to do with a person's knowledge and experience — skills you develop from doing the job in the past. Commitment is made up of confidence and motivation. Confidence involves the self awareness related to believing that you can do the job, while motivation is *voluntary* enthusiasm to do the job.

Blanchard describes four levels of competence and commitment:

D1 Low competence, but the high enthusiasm characteristic of the enthusiastic beginner — which requires a *directing style* — explaining how, what, when and where to do the task.

D2 Where people have some competence, but low commitment (motivation or confidence). This person needs both direction and support and therefore *coaching* is the appropriate style.

D3 The third developmental level, comprising of a person with high competence and variable commitment, requires listening, motivation and a *supportive* leadership style.

D4 Finally, the highest developmental level — a person who has high competence and commitment calls for delegation on the part of the leader. The art of 'growing people' then is to diagnose people's present developmental level, and then to help them move to become committed and competent (D4).

The example of someone learning to play golf illustrates the process toward empowerment and the leader's role in this regard. The enthusiastic beginner goes to a golfing pro to take lessons. The professional starts with directing the person by telling them what to do, how to hold the club etc. After a few lessons, invariably the 'handicap of golf' takes its toll and our commitment decines as we realise that the game is harder than it looks.

A good professional will notice this drop in motivation and adopt a coaching style — to help the learner persevere. At the third developmental level — the professional primarily provides 'psychological support' as the learner has mastered the technical aspects of the game. Finally, the good professional will delegate responsibility to the learner to go out and practice alone. If he/she has done his/her job correctly — the competent golfer will be able to independently diagnose and correct his/her game in future. This example illustrates the role of the leader in providing for the learner what the learner cannot provide for him/herself.

Matching leadership styles with people's competence prevents the typical problems of under-supervision where one is frustrated because one has unrealistic expectations, and over-supervision where one frustrates one's people.

The final but essential skill of leadership is discussing, agreeing and *contracting* with followers as to how you will operate as a leader. Contracting starts with clear goal setting for each of the follower's specific tasks. Developmental level is task specific and may *differ* with respect to *each* key performance area.

The leader analyses and discusses with followers their developmental level and consequently the expectations of the appropriate leadership style. This *must* be translated into specific actions where learning can take place on a regular basis. The leader also needs to maintain regular contact in order to *observe* performance and adjust the leadership style accordingly. Consequently, the process of empowerment takes time and commitment from the leader, who in turn must be recognised and rewarded for the effort.

✦

CHAPTER X

EXPLAINING EFFECTIVE AND INEFFECTIVE LEADERSHIP

INTRODUCTION

Kouzes and Posner point out that leader self studies reveal only half of the essence of leadership. A leader, by definition, must have followers who choose to follow him/her. In this regard, leadership is in the eye of the follower or the experience followers have of leadership activity.[1] Consequently, it is not the intention of the leader that is important, but the *follower's experience* of this behaviour that will determine the action that is taken, and thus the effectiveness of leadership. In this regard, the extent of perceptual overlap between leaders and followers is vital for effective leadership.

Hersey and Blanchard comment on the importance of a leadership that is flexible and able to adapt to a variety of situational demands and follower expectations.[2] Comparing one's self perception of leadership with perceptions of others is essential, particularly since one's self perceptions may not reflect actual leadership behaviour, depending on the degree of perceptual overlap with others.

Results from the South African research show significant differences between average leader self-perceptions and follower perceptions of the same leadership activity. In contrast, there was no difference between the perceptions of excellent leaders and their followers. Overall, excellent leaders had a mean self-rating score of 177,10 compared to the 175,70 scored by their followers on the leadership competence questionnaire. In contrast, the average leaders' self-score of 168,10

105

differed significantly with the 112,70 mean of their followers. A similar significant difference of vastly divergent perceptions occurred on all five competence dimensions, between average leaders and their followers.[3]

Consequently, the critical variable in measuring leadership is followers who experience the impact of leadership behaviour. 'Average leaders' are not aware of the negative impact they are having and consequently there is a perceptual gap between leader intentions and follower experiences.

How does one explain the divergent perceptions of 'average leaders and followers' and more importantly how does one begin to narrow this perceptual gap?

PERCEPTUAL CONGRUENCE

Perceptions are the mental image created through sensory impressions of events in the internal world. Its base is past experience which can be accurate, inaccurate, negative or positive. Needs, beliefs, emotions and expectations all affect the way we construct our perceptual world and therefore our sensory evidence is not always reliable.[4]

Perception is a 'mental model' of the individual's view of the world. Rules, conventions, norms, stereotypes and attitudes all govern the way the individual believes he/she sees, and we impose our own structure on what we see. We tend to organise information in a way that is predictable and makes sense into a perceptual set.[5]

Consequently, the reason why fundamental change is not embraced by many people could be that it requires changed perceptions, or a changed world view before constructive action is taken. In the absence of perceived competence, many people retreat toward the stability and comfort of that which is known often to the detriment of personal and organisational growth.

Leadership as a change process, of necessity must clarify self-perceptions and the perceptions of others in order to provide a basis for co-ordinated activity. As Bennis and Nanus point out, all organisations depend on the existence of shared meanings and interpretations of reality which facilitate co-ordinated action.[6]

Consequently, much of the worldwide commitment and credibility problems facing organisational leaders is of their own making, because of the divergent perception of leaders and their constituents. Leaders have failed to instil meaning, trust and empowerment in their followers, because they are *out of touch with themselves and the people they serve.* The primary reason then for a loss of credibility is leadership that is insensitive to its constituents.

Mark McCormack concurs, pointing out that performance problems often stem from a disparity between a manager and his/her subordinate's perception of key job priorities.[7]

In essence, distorted perceptions occur because leaders don't apply refined interpersonal skills and operate from an egocentric perspective rather than as a steward in the service of others. This relates to the abuse of power for self gain in service of self and consequent mistrust in constituents.

In contrast, the leadership competence of self-management involves the ability to recognise strengths and to compensate for weaknesses, including an eagerness to get feedback concerning performance and the impact your behaviour is having on others. This includes the realisation that reality for constituents is their perception of events rather than the intention of the leader. Shared perceptions also involve leaders who have the sensory awareness to identify activity that is not working and accordingly accepting personal responsibility for change, rather than blaming other people.

Distorted perceptions indicate a failure to demonstrate the competencies of accurate self assessment described by Boyatsis — perceptual objectivity which includes having a realistic grounded view of self, and ability to be relatively objective, rather than being limited by excessive subjectivity or personal biases. Shared perceptions also require an element of self control or the ability to inhibit personal needs in service of organisational goals.[8]

FEEDBACK — THE BREAKFAST OF CHAMPIONS

In the early seventies Joseph Luft and Harry Ingham developed an instrument known as the Johari Window, designed to measure the extent to which people give and receive verbal *and non-verbal* feedback. They point out that there are some attitudes and behaviours engaged in by leaders that they know about themselves. This 'known to self area' included their knowledge of the way they are coming across to the people whom they are trying to influence. At the same time, part of the leader's personality is 'unknown to self' and the impact they have on others. This could be due to their followers not giving them feedback or due to the leader not being sufficiently alert to pick up and comprehend the verbal and non-verbal environmental clues.

There will also be parts of the leader's personality that are known to other people that he/she is not aware of (blind spot), as well as the private area which he/she is aware of but does not disclose to other people. The arena that is known to self and is disclosed to others is referred to as the 'public arena', while that area that both the leader and others are not aware of has been labelled the 'unknown'. This unconscious area may be having a relevant and dramatic impact in terms of choices of activity and the way this impacts on others.[9]

Hersey and Blanchard comment from extensive leadership research involving the Johari Window, that it is possible to predict the shape of the public arena. If there is a great discrepancy between leader self perception and follower's perception, the leader's public arena would tend to be very small. The converse applies with a large arena where significant perceptual overlap occurs.[10] Consequently, we would expect average leaders in this study to have a narrow arena due to extensive psychological defences and an organisational culture that does not encourage the giving and receiving of feedback, particularly from subordinates.

There are two processes that affect the shape of the Johari Window, or configuration of the above four areas. The first is called *receiving feedback* — the extent to which others in the organisational setting are willing to share with the leader on how he or she is coming across. This is also dependent on the degree of trust in the organisation and the degree of openness in the organisational culture to challenge the status quo and to learn from mistakes. It also requires openness or willingness from the leader to perceive this feedback. This willingness is in turn related to an internal locus of control or 'assuming responsiblity to initiate and sustain change'.

The willingness to *receive feedback* is also related to the following leadership competencies:

❑ Seeks to understand what is preventing an organisation or department from growing and achieving its objectives.
❑ Is able to diagnose and change inappropriate behaviour and independently take constructive action.
❑ Accepts responsibility for creating individual life experience, rather than blaming situations or people for misfortune.
❑ Perceives change and threatening situations as a challenge and opportunity for personal and/or organisational growth.
❑ Is committed to self development and continual learning.

Excellent leaders were scored significantly higher on all of the above, by their followers, in contrast to follower scores of average leaders. Many managers cut off and effectively stifle feedback from their people by arguing with them about their feelings and perceptions, not being able to draw the distinction between unacceptable feelings and unacceptable behaviour.

In contrast, successful people realise that 'feedback is the breakfast of champions' and is the only way for people to learn, adapt and grow. Feedback which is negative is construed by successful people as an opportunity to try something new, and not as failure — with the consequent employment of defences to protect a weak self concept. Warren Bennis concurs, pointing out that leaders encourage dissent, or the organisational corollary of reflective backtalk, 'Leaders need people around them who have contrary views, who are devil's advocates, and variance sensors who can tell them the difference between what is expected and what is going on.'[11]

STRAIGHT FEEDBACK — CONGRUENCE IN WORD AND DEED

The second process affecting the shape of a person's Johari Window is the process of *disclosure or giving feedback*. This involves the extent to which leaders are willing to share with others in their organisational setting, data about themselves, their feelings, attitudes and assumptions. In the process of disclosure, the more organisationally relevant information the leaders disclose, the more the public arena opens up, and followers themselves can make *informed decisions* about how to act more effectively.

Hersey and Blanchard confirm the process of increased self awareness:

'An interesting phenomenon occurs in settings where there is simultaneous feedback and disclosure. Not only does the public arena of these leaders begin to extend itself into the blind and private arenas, but there is also the high possibility that some of what was previously unknown will begin to surface into the public arena.'[12]

This practice of giving and receiving feedback which is a vital instrument to both the psychotherapist and organisational development specialist, of necessity involves an element of risk and rejection. Giving and receiving feedback involves identifying where an organisation now stands in relation to its objectives, and identifying the self defeating patterns and learning disabilities preventing organisational and individual growth.

In summary, then, the key to obtaining a perceptual fit between leaders and followers appears to be the leader's willingness and ability to manage him/herself by receiving and giving feedback.

Amongst South African executives Kelly found that leadership was essentially an interpersonal activity including the importance of being in touch with one's people, of being able to communicate with them, empower them and draw them in behind one. Self awareness and congruence in word and deed are critical factors underpinning the above.[13]

On an international level, Boyatsis found that the competencies of effective self management were significantly related to self assessment, self control, concern with impact and self confidence as criteria underpinning managerial success.[14]

Warren Bennis summarises the importance of self awareness and other competencies in developing complementary leader-follower perceptions:

'Leadership development is based on the assumption that leaders are people who are able to express themselves fully. By this I mean that they know who they are, what their strengths and weaknesses are, and how to fully deploy their strengths and compensate for their weaknesses.

They also know what they want, why they want it, and how to communicate what they want to others, in order to gain their cooperation
and support.

'Finally they know how to achieve their goals. The key to full self-expression is understanding one's self and the world, and the key to
understanding is learning — from one's own life and experience.'[15]

LEADERSHIP IS LEARNING

The difference between successful and unsuccessful leadership can be summed up in one word — learning. Leaders,
despite the organisational culture, have learned the competencies of leadership the hard way — through trial and
error. This process of learning is described below by South
African executives.

'I had to learn to be more sensitive in my dealings with people.'
(Executive number 5)

'I learnt that you can't play around with people as if they're pawns. If
somehow a trust relationship breaks, you can't easily fix it.'
(Executive number 25)

'Being self-taught, I'm a very hands-on manager. I had to learn to allow
people to do it their own way. I had to learn to allow them to make their
own mistakes.'
(Executive number 20)[16]

Lifelong learning is a fundamental vehicle for leadership.
Bennis points out that leaders have learnt to overcome typical
learning disabilities where what we need to know gets lost in
what we are told we should know. Learning, then, is simply
a case of remembering what is important.

'This process of learning has many recurrent themes — the need for
education both formal and informal, the need to unlearn so that you can
learn (overcoming self defeating patterns of behaviour), the need for
reflecting on learning so that the meaning of the lesson is understood,
the need to take risks, make mistakes, and the need for competence, for
mastery of the task at hand.'

Bennis distinguishes between the once-born and twice-born
leader and learner. The first group has an easy transition
through life and has become a product of their circumstances.

In contrast, the twice-borns are often isolated or suffer in the developmental process, learning to become independent, relying wholly on their own beliefs and ideas.

Consequently, the twice-born leaders have learnt what works for them, and to commit themselves to follow their own inner voice in order to express themselves fully, regardless of the context.[17]

Because leadership is the axiom behind any successful organisation, it is too important to 'hope the exceptional few' will cultivate competencies over a lifetime. How, given the failure of management education previously described, can leadership be developed in a way that significantly impacts on organisational performance?

THE 'KEYS' TO LEARNING

A recent *Sunday Star* article on Derek Keys, the Government's new Minister of Trade and Industry and Finance, illustrates the importance of empowerment and learning — in his own leadership development process.[14] Keys points to the importance of having an opportunity to learn and prove himself at the age of 29 — to mastermind Safmarine's thrust into global markets — as being one of the highlights of his career. The 'vast stores of knowledge' derived from heading up National Discount House where 'I learnt precisely what makes the economy tick', were also invaluable.

In addition the experience as a business consultant, and then as head of Gencor were invaluable learning experiences:

❏ His stint as a business consultant helped him come to grips with a wide variety of economic issues and, perhaps more importantly, acquire the interpersonal skills required for dealing with hard-nosed entrepeneurs.

'More often then not I knew what they needed to do, though they had different ideas. If I didn't get the point across the first time, I tried a different approach; if that didn't work, I tried another — until eventually the penny dropped.'

❏ His spell as head of Gencor, where he ascribes his well-documented successes largely to the fact that he never issued any orders or instructions.

'All major decisions were based on consultation, discussion and deliberation. I was merely a facilitator — a kind of father figure who offered suggestions and recommendations.'

Mr Keys greatest obstacle may be getting co-operation from his Cabinet colleagues.

He isn't concerned: 'I've dealt reasonably well with all manner of people all my life. There's no reason for me to expect otherwise in the years that lie ahead.'

The importance of focussing attention was also underscored by Keys in coping with and introducing change:

'I tend to compartmentalise problem areas and sort them out one by one. If the problem horison becomes too wide, I lose interest.'

In essence Keys views his new challenge as a 'post retirement *service* to the South African community' that will require long hours and much dedication as well as optimism that these problems can be solved.[14]

✦
STRATEGIC LEADERSHIP DEVELOPMENT

INTRODUCTION

I can hear the chorus of the sceptics doubting whether leadership can be taught. They do have a point, given the failure of both formal and informal education to deliver, and the multitude of restraining factors hindering organisational and individual change. This, however, could also be an excuse for not changing their own leadership behaviour and committing their organisations to strategic leadership development.

CAN THE ORGANISATIONAL LEOPARD CHANGE ITS SPOTS?

The first issue to clarify is — *change from what to what?* Change needs to occur from the managerial spots indelibly linked to the hierarchical organisation that produces conditioned responders, to a 'leader-leopard' that eats change for breakfast and inspires other organisational animals in the process.

The leader-leopard, as a social animal, transforms the hearts and minds of other 'animals' in a way that the individuality of the animal remains, and the lamb can lie down with the lion because they both need one another to fulfil their potential

115

The next question to confront is — *can* the leopard change? The answer, it appears, depends on the position from which you view the leopard:

❏ The organisational development and strategy people will probably answer to the negative unless the person in question meets a bolt of lightening on the road to Damascus — which is a fairly expensive exercise!

❏ Eugene the albino lion will probably say 'over my dead body — once a leopard, always a leopard; White leopards stay in Londolozi or Oranjesicht, while Black leopards stay in Soweto!'

❏ Nelson, the wise owl, shakes his head sadly and says 'I have lived with this animal all my life and change will only occur if you apply pressure through sanctions and the like — and it all depends on the leopards support.'

❏ Inkatha will point out that they have been a non-violent leopard all along — and change will only occur if you involve key people in the process.

❏ The Nationalist Party will point out that now the change process is irreversible (the Yes vote), and that we need foreign investment to help support change.

❏ The business world points out that free enterprise and capitalism are genetic prescriptions for the leopard and other animals to live in harmony — but watch out for the unions!

In desperation, I sought the advice of two experts on the subject — The Mad Hatter and Oom Schalk Lourens. Oom Schalk Lourens, at Abjaterskop, was involved in detailed research of leopards long before it was fashionable to wear veldskoens. He points out that in his case, the leopard was intensely curious and did not give in to his natural instinct to eat people.[1] So you see, *it all depends on the environment of the leopard.* If he is allowed to survive and develop to his/her full potential, it is possible for him to peacefully co-exist with, and even add value to the rest of the animal kingdom.

At the end of our conversation, Oom Schalk ran his fingers over his balding head and concluded on a sad note that the magnificent animal had been shot by farmers who feared that it would destroy their animal wealth.

I reflected on this prophetic warning, and remembered the threat of extinction that hangs over the *leader* leopard — who is often labelled as a rebel or a maverick and seen as being disloyal — particularly if there are *managers* above him/her in the organisational hierarchy.

The other issue that stuck in my mind, after talking to Oom Schalk, was whether the organisation was 'environmentally friendly' to the leopard, and I remembered the old saying, 'a prophet in his own town . . . '. After much soul searching, I have wrestled with and concluded the questions of change as follows:

❑ *Does the Leopard Need to Change?*

Environmental trends impacting on organisations demanding increased competitiveness, indicate that business has no alternative but to liberate human resources through leadership, or join the kwagga in extinction.

❑ *Is the Leopard Capable of Changing?*

Evidence from South Africa's top business leaders points to a resounding 'yes'. All recognised South African leaders comment that their *ability to learn to lead* was a fundamental criteria underpinning business success.[2] Hersey and Blanchard summarise recent thinking by pointing out that leadership competence can be learnt, but question the willingness of people to learn to become adaptable.[3]

❑ *Does the Leopard Want to Change?*

This is the crucial question. The answer, I believe, is a matter of individual choice. Certainly people will be more prepared to take 'the road less travelled' if they have signposts — in the form of leadership training and support on the way.

Let us be certain on this point. If people pay lip service to the concept of leadership and empowerment, they must be allowed the consequences of their actions — being left behind by the organisation, incurring the wrath of the CEO, being out of touch with their followers and ultimately going out of business. We need to remember that it is the leader and not the manager that is the protected species — so make the penalties for not changing tough — because it's bad for business!

Once people are conscious of the impact they are having on others, both clinical experience and extensive organisational development research have shown that behaviour can be altered if people are willing to do so. Consequently, feedback to people concerning the 'perceptual gap differential' with followers is a vital *precursor* to obtaining commitment to change.

No growth will occur until people have personalised the need to change by confronting or being confronted with the question: *How do I contribute to the problem?*

Finally, Oom Schalk leaned forward with an elbow resting on a calloused knee and looked me straight in the eye. 'At the end of the day there are a couple of criteria that underpin any attempts to grow the leader leopard,' he said:

❏ Identifying and removing organisational obstacles to learning and growth
❏ Change will only occur if a learning and empowering culture is developed, enabling 'human leopards' to grow.
❏ There will inevitably be resistance to change which threatens peoples security. Be prepared, and understand this. Give people a choice — spell out the benefits for them — and it they still do not perform — take action.

❏ There needs to be a holistic strategic approach to developing leadership.

BEYOND THE QUICK FIX

Change on an individual level is difficult enough. Permanent change on an *organisational level* demands attention to a multitude of factors that have to be aligned before the hurdle of resistance is overcome.

Change, from an ecological perspective means that an intervention in one part of the system i.e. training or strategy, will have a reverberation effect throughout the organisation. Human beings, just like natural systems, vacilate between stability and change. This means that change will often be met with a pull towards stability. Consequently, organisational change needs a multifaceted strategic approach, complimenting change at different levels of the organisation. Change has to be viewed from an holistic systems approach where change in one part of the system, will have a reverberating effect throughout the organisation — which needs to be anticipated. People also need to be trained in the 'process competencies' underpinning successful change, which are illustrated on the following page.

I have included a Table (on page 121), summarising the *why, what and how of effective strategic development* in general — given the failures of informal management development in South Africa.[4] The need for development is summarised in the first column, followed by a summary of the reasons behind the failure of formal and informal management development. This gives rise for the need for a systematic holistic strategic approach to human resource development and the objective of *getting the right people, in the right place, at the right time.*

Lastly, specific recommendations or critical leverage areas are offered in order to counteract the problems described above — and are elaborated on in this chapter.

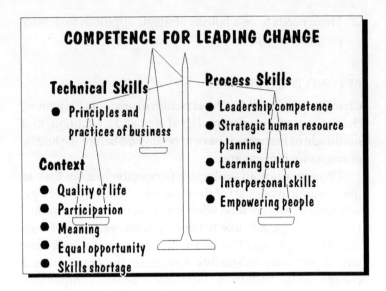

ORGANISATIONAL BUILDING BLOCKS

The following factors are essential to the strategic development and implementation of leadership:

1. *Strategic business plan*
The Strategic Business Plan provides a starting point for any development of leadership and empowerment. The business plan is a map for gaining and/or retaining an organisation's competitive advantage. This presupposes an understanding of the critical issues in the environment surrounding the business and 'catering' for them by adopting certain strategies:

I will use the Chamber of Mines as a practical example, of an organisation that has committed itself to developing leadership and implementing equal opportunity.

The Chamber of Mines of South Africa is a private enterprise service organisation which was set up in 1898 to pro-

Table 11.1
STRATEGIC DEVELOPMENT — LEADERSHIP & EMPOWERMENT

WHY DEVELOPMENT	FAILURE OF MANAGEMENT DEVELOPMENT	FAILURE OF INFORMAL DEVELOPMENT IN SA (Pruett)	OBJECTIVE STRATEGIC DEVELOPMENT	CRITICAL FOCUS

• Burgeoning skills shortage
• Demand for personal growth, participation, quality of life
• Quality of people — primary source of competitive advantage
• Human development — axiom behind successful nations, organisations
• Learning Race — key to growth
• **Leadership — key to:**
  – skills shortage
  – workers' needs
  – human development
  – learning race
  – change and growth
  – productivity
• Focus on leadership — *not* management development
	• Failure of business schools — miseducation and focus on technical skills
	• **Critical C.E.O. success factors**
	  – Leadership
	  – Interpersonal and motivational skills
	  – In touch with people
	  – Empowerment
	  – Hard work
	
	Leadership is a learning process with 5 core competencies:
	  – Vision
	  – Meaning/Communication
	  – Trust
	  – Self-management
	  – Empowerment
		• Irrelevant material
		• Follow fads
		• Skills not attitude-focused
		• Produce 'conditioned' responders
		• Lack of trainer competence
		• No follow-up or transfer of skills to work place
		• Lack of line-manager support
		• Piecemeal approach — not strategic
		• No model of competence and success
			• Holistic multifaceted approach
			• Systems approach — a change in one part of the system will have a reverberating effect
			• The identification of needed skills and competence, and active management of employee learning for the *long range* future, in relation to specific corporate strategies
			• Objective: 'To get the right people, in the right place, at the right time.'
				• Guided by business plan
				• Human resource strategy — identify competencies underpinning success
				• Organisational development — learning culture
				• Strategic selection
				• Follower appraisals
				• Strategic rewards
				• C.E.O. support
				• Creative training methodology that impacts on bottom line
				• Generate commitment — personalise the need for leadership
				• Training for leadership, learning and change
				• Simultaneously 'bottom-up' equal opportunity focus

mote and protect the interests of the South African mining industry. The mission of the Chamber, is to provide a variety of advisory and service functions, which can most effectively be handled on a central co-operative basis, by:

1. Maintaining close contact with the mining industry, and anticipating and identifying those areas where collaborative services would be beneficial.

2. The advancement, protection and promotion of the mutual interests and common requirements agreed by members.

3. The provision of *leadership* and representation in matters of industry concern, in both national and international affairs.

4. The maintenance of expertise and excellence in areas of importance to the industry.

5. The co-ordination of industry activities.

6. The promotion of activities which result in reduced costs to mines (Chamber of Mines Strategic Plan, 1990).[5]

The 1991 Chamber of Mines Management Conference — convened to assess past and to develop future strategy was characterised by the themes of change, and a depressed gold mining industry with an estimated retrenchment of 45 000 employees in 1990/91. This is likely to impact on the Chamber with calls for greater leadership (external and internal) than at any other time in the history of the organisation. Emphasis was placed on service excellence, marketing, upgrading staff skills and expertise, and maintaining and expanding the customer base as key success factors contributing to competitive advantage[6] (C.E.O. address — Management Conference, 1991).

The Chamber, like any other organisation, is directly dependent on the quality of its human resources to achieve its objectives. In this respect, it is competing with other organisations, to develop and train existing staff, and to recruit qualified people. To exacerbate the demand and supply problem the business environment is characterised by a skills shortage, a demand for equal opportunity, and expectations of quality of life and participation. These can be summarised as a need to empower people, which in turn demands effective transformational leadership to meet these challenges.

However, despite the documented need to provide industry leaders and maintain industry expertise and leadership, little formal strategic development had taken place prior to 1989. This illustrates the gap between strategic formulation and implementation. At the same time, political changes — including 'talk' of nationalisation — as well as the country's escalating skills shortage — hastened the need to embark on an equal opportunity programme primarily involving the human resource department and, more specifically, the training centre. From the above, it is clear that leadership which provides focus during exponential change and empowers people to be more productive, takes on a fundamental strategic focus.

2. Human resource strategy — identify competencies underpinning success

The human resource strategy takes its direction from the overall business plan. The H.R. plan consists primarily of four interrelated components: selection, appraisal, development and rewards. The right people need to be selected, based on the identified competencies essential to the job; they need to be appraised in terms of these competencies and specific performance objectives; training and development then takes place in terms the identified gaps and weaknesses revealed by the appraisal; and, finally, on the basis of performance, rewards are allocated. These four components are consequently dependent on *identifying specific competencies underpinning organisational success* and hence the need to identify exactly what constitutes a good leader in a particular organisation.

These competencies also guide any organisational development interventions in an attempt to create an environment conducive to the *application* of essential skills that underpin and improve bottom line performance. In terms of the two critical strategic issues — leadership and empowerment/equal opportunity, a learning organisation culture is mandatory.

3. *Organisational development — toward a learning organisation*
As previously discussed, the critical factor distinguishing average from excellent leadership, is the ability to learn on the job.[7] Consequently, anything and anyone who inhibits learning should be removed. For most organisations, this means a radical change from the status orientated hierarchical organisation with its rigidity and power struggles, to an environment that promotes learning and enables people to perform to the maximum of their ability.

Peter Senge, describes five fundamental disciplines of the learning organisation, which are remarkably similar to the five competencies of effective leadership identified in my research: vision; personal mastery; mental models; team learning and systems thinking.

Senge's first discipline is building shared vision; while the need for 'personal mastery', identifying appropriate 'mental models' and 'systems thinking' are fundamental to the effective management of self. The discipline of 'team learning' involves people being aligned around a common purpose, and the ability to learn together in an environment that allows for the free flow of discussion and meaning . This relates to the leadership competence of 'the management of meaning through communication and the importance of creating an empowering or learning environment'.

Leadership then, is inextricably linked to a learning organisation. Arie de Geus, underscores the importance of developing a learning organisation and the fundamental role of the leader:

'Our exploration into the area of institutional learning is not a luxury. We understand that the only competitive advantage the company of the future will have is its managers' ability to learn faster than their competitors. So the companies that succeed will be those that continually nudge their managers towards revising their views of the world. The challenges for the planner are as considerable. So are the rewards' (De Geus 1991, Centre for Innovative Leadership Brochure)

Any attempts to develop leadership and implement equal opportunity without creating a learning environment with management attitudes conducive to development, will simply be empowering people to leave the organisation.

Consequently, organisational development needs to occur *concurrently* with any training and this necessitates taking a hard look at where the organisation is now, and where it needs to be in order to align itself with an exponentially changing environment. Thus the decision is based on pragmatic business sense and not a 'do-gooder humanitarian feeling'.

The emphasis in the 90' s of necessity, needs to be on developing leaders, who in turn can develop a learning culture. This indicates a need for organisational development and management development to merge. The first step on this path, I believe, is the development of leadership. Once there is a common competence and language in an organisation — more formal organisation development can occur as part of the change process.

4. Strategic selection

Underpinning the strategic development of leadership, is the selection of people, ideally with the *present* ability to display leadership competence. The leadership competence questionnaire used for the South African leadership research and described throughout this book, is a useful, time saving method of identifying leadership skills. However, care should be taken to get at least two unbiased follower ratings in addition to the leader rating.

The person doing the selection can ask the followers directly for their 'leader rating' and consequently guarantee anonymity and confidentiality. The twenty-five competencies distinguishing excellent leaders, in addition to selection criteria, form a useful starting point for organisations to identify objective performance measurement and appraisal criteria. These should be discussed and tailored to suit the organisations specific circumstances. The rule of thumb is: test the competencies, discuss them, if they are valid use them, if not, adapt the competencies or throw them out!

5. Follower appraisal
The research clearly showed that the only way to measure leadership effectively is from a follower perspective — the people who experience the leadership behaviour. I'm well aware that this goes against the grain as most organisation have a 'superior' assessment or performance review — and occasionally this is extended to include peers.

However, an interesting change occurs when the boss suddenly realises that he is accountable to his staff, who now hold a key to his future career aspirations. Suddenly he is doing everything she/he can to create an empowering work environment, and if people are going to experience this as genuine, he has no option but to adopt a 'servant attitude' to leadership, and become accountable to followers. It is suggested that some of the competencies identified in the South African leadership research form the basis of a follower review and used together with other methods of appraisal.

6. *Strategic rewards*

Because leadership is the axiom behind successful organisations or business units of any size, specific competencies should — after discussion and consent — be used as a basis to reward people. Any reward structure must be sufficiently flexible to distinguish between excellent and below average performers to encourage exceptional effort. This in turn should be linked to an organisations bottom line which in the case of service organisations must be more than simply cutting costs and include quantitative and qualitative measurement criteria.

One little, but not unimportant, point: The allocation of rewards must be equitable — as perceived by people who are being rewarded. Despite herculeon attempts by organisations to keep their bonuses and salaries secret — people in organisations actually talk to one another. If they discover inconsistencies in the way in which rewards are allocated, this will become an instant demotivator.

Finally, we need to create incentives *throughout* the organisation and not only rewarding the boss, or people above a certain grade. By this traditional method, organisations are perpetuating the myth of the Lone Ranger cowboy hero who leads from the front and whose success has nothing to do with a team effort.

7. *CEO Support*

Any change management and developmental programme is only as good as the chief executive officers support. This translates to absolute commitment to leadership and becoming a congruent role model to drive home the need for change. This demands time, energy and visibility — and two-way communication to get and give direct feedback on peoples progress in implementing leadership competencies. You cannot delegate this commitment. Not having enough time is never an excuse — one is simply saying that I choose to spend my time on different things.

One organisation I consulted with pointed out that the top people in the company spent 80 % of their time on external matters which took them away from the office on a regular basis. Yet they were still responsible for the performance and motivation of the business — an impossible task to do effectively if you are not there to apply the competencies of leadership. Apart from anything else, these 'foreigners' have the power to make changes and very often responsibility but not authority is delegated.

When I questioned the rationale behind this state of affairs, I was told that it was the only way the organisation could retain the services of these busy executives. They would leave if they could not continue practising the enjoyable pursuits of the job. Granted, we all need to enjoy our work, but not at the expense of other people who depend on us for leadership. Either the leader consults full-time in a one-man-band, or he devotes his energy to motivating people and creating an empowering environment.

Lastly, the CEO must hold people accountable and take action against people who resist change; do not apply effective leadership, and consequently underperform. A gentle word in the pub after work or at the annual strategic retreat is nowhere as effective as visibly coming down hard on people who do not deliver.

8. Creative training methodology that impacts on bottom line
If training cannot be shown to directly impact on peoples ability to perform more productively, then it is a waste of time.

This requires competent trainers who are schooled in the dynamics underpinning individual and organisational change, as well as 'process training' and the ability to impact on both an *attitudinal* and a skills level. Training offers a critical leverage point for organisational growth[8], and human resource and training professionals are increasingly going to be called on to provide direction on people issues in the boardroom. In short, the trainers need to be leaders in their own right and work on both a strategic and an operational level to deliver the goods. They also need to understand the language of business and the principles underpinning adult learning.

If we do not add value to an organisations human resources, then we do not deserve to be taken seriously. This in turn necessitates getting close to line managers to find out what 'goods' need to be delivered.

Leadership training is most effective when the entire management team attend a course together. During my leadership training course, for example, the team is required to continually apply the leadership competencies: first individually, and then as a team that jointly clarify their vision, develop strategies to create meaning and intrinsic motivation at work; develop communication strategies; identify obstacles to trust and empowerment and their individual strengths and weaknesses in managing themselves, together with a commitment to improve on these.

The four-day training course (described in detail towards the end of this chapter) is split into two days each, with a two week break inbetween. The team is required to implement the leadership competencies during the course break, and during a follow-up to *demonstrate* their application on the job. The follow-up also allows an opportunity for people to share their experiences during implementation. Before and during the process of implementation, the trainer/consultant needs to be available to deal with issues that arise and to maintain the momentum generated during training.

It is also vital that organisations adopt ownership of any leadership development — through a train-the-trainer process which is then cascaded down the organisation. However, while this is vital for line and organisational ownership, it is not always possible to find the right champions or trainers to cope with the complex programme.

I suggest that prospective trainers should be selected both in terms of their commitment to the course, and their ability to train effectively. The process then includes an additional four day train-the-trainer process together with a phased in live presentation of the course, with the trainer present. Another difficulty arises due to the fairly complex nature of the material and the need to think in a systems, rather than a linear cause-effect manner. Any course should, however, be adapted to the needs and the level of the trainers.

9. *Generate Commitment — Personalise the Need for Leadership Competence*

A vital adjunct to training is the need for people to personalise responsibility for change. The easiest way to do this is to administer a leadership competence questionnaire to both leader (self) and followers (rating the leader) *prior to any intervention.* Thereafter, feedback needs to be skilfully given, pointing out perceptual incongruities and the consequence to the leader and the department. In essence then, a need is created prior to training.

This evaluation and feedback process needs to be delicately handled and may evolve into a stress management — even therapeutic — encounter, given the fact that South African managers are the most stressed in the world.[9] People may also need to be destressed through empathetic listening and reflecting, prior to and during training, otherwise, they will employ an elaborate range of defences and will not be able to 'hear' anything, let alone see how they are contributing to the problem. This process is also vital in building up a trusting relationship with people who feel that the trainer understands the nature of their business. The empathetic process is also essential for the training consultant to earn the right to continually challenge people.

Measuring competencies should occur throughout training, leaving people with a very clear idea of their strengths and weaknesses on each of the five leadership competencies.

The following graphic demonstrates the process of obtaining organisational and individual commitment to the leadership and change process.

LEADERSHIP COMPETENCE DEVELOPMENT

Process

- Measure existing competence - leadership questionnaire
- Individual feedback — establish commitment
  — Gather information
  — De-stress people
- Programme based on developmental needs
- Market/get support for programme
  — CEO support — reward and consequence
- Training — management team

10. Training for Leadership, Learning and Change

I have included an example of my leadership training programme as a guide to course development within organisations.

LEADERSHIP COMPETENCE DEVELOPMENT

Process

● On-the-job application — 1 day follow up
● Train the trainer cascade (line ownership)
● Ongoing support
● Adopt systems to compliment (evaluation/reward)
● Self sufficient — transfer ownership

Objective:

To produce competent leadership activity that significantly impacts on organisational growth and productivity.

The content covers the following strategic and operational issues:

❑ A South African leadership case study.
❑ The evolving context of business and 'people issues' affecting an organisations leadership.
❑ The nature of human motivation and productivity and the leader's role and specific behaviour in developing people and optimising their potential.
❑ To identify leadership competencies from a leader and a follower perspective, thereby arriving at learning objectives that can be measured.
❑ The stragegic development and implementation of
   • Vision
   • Communication and intrinsic motivation

- Trust
- The management of self
- Empowerment

❏ Theory and practice of the learning organisation.

❏ Understanding individual and organisational change and operationalising principles underpinning growth and change.

❏ Application of competencies on the job.

Each individual and team is required to apply learning at work and to demonstrate competence during a day follow-up after training.

11. Equal Opportunity — Bottom Up

'Equal opportunity is not an option, it is a strategic must. Not only does it help to create a more equalised society, but it also ensures continuity of the free enterprise system. The road is not an easy one, but after the effort will emerge the benefits of wealth creation.'[10]

One of the major problems confronting managers daily, is the burgeoning skills shortage, exacerbated by the fact that people entering the job market from school or university do not always have the skills necessary to add value to the business.

Consequently, if organisations are to survive a determined persistent programme aimed at the upward mobility of and advancement of Black people and women into *real* managerial positions, is mandatory.

Any leadership programme, which is essentially a top-down strategy, needs to be complemented by a strategic bottom-up thrust to compliment equal opportunity. Indeed, the two strategies compliment and reinforce one another because part of leadership is empowerment — a vital component of equal opportunity.

Attention to both strategic thrusts creates an opportunity for both leaders and followers to take responsibility — now that they have the competence. Consequently, there can be no excuse for not producing the goods, and those people who do not perform will have to leave the organisation.

In summary then, the Strategic Development and Implementation of Leadership is represented in the figure below.

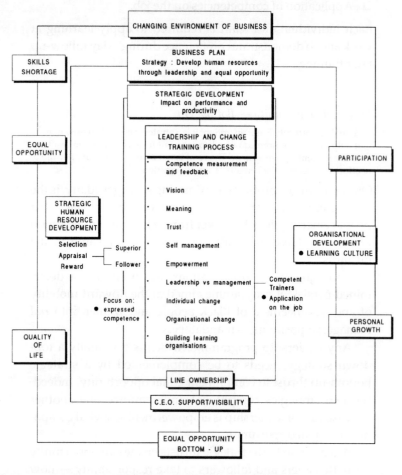

STRATEGIC LEADERSHIP DEVELOPMENT

EPILOGUE

As previously mentioned, this book is intended as a catalyst toward the further development of leadership within South African organisations. There are, to date, a few organisations — such as the Centre for Innovative Leadership (Louis van der Merwe), progressive business schools, authors and individuals — who have taken up this challenge.

However, although these pathfinders have taken the road less travelled — their journeys cannot accommodate passengers coming along for the ride. South Africa, indeed the world, needs a fundamentally different approach to create transformational leaders. We need to couple attempts at improving education, literacy, productivity, management, quality and equal opportunity with leadership which offers a fundamental leverage for second order change.

If human competence is to become a reality, we need:

❑ To start developing, reorganising and rewarding leadership as part of a broad educational strategy.
❑ Make human skills and people management an integral part of every university or post matric learning process.
❑ Trainers, educators, line managers, professionals of any persuasion need to commit themselves to become competent trainers of leadership (with standards of excellence maintained).
❑ Extensive research that focuses on a broader leadership sample together with researching the leaders role in em-

powerment, equal opportunity, culture and motivation —
in a way that lends itself to practical application.

❏ Leadership development programmes that are tried-and-
tested and shared, particularly in a Third World context.

❏ Centres of 'learning for leadership' be established, catering for a variety of students from political, business, cultural, religious and even sporting organisations — with a
commitment to follow-up and implementation of competencies.

REFERENCES

Introduction
1. Moss-Kanter, R 1983. *The Change Masters — Corporate Entrepreneurs at Work.* London: Unwin Paperbacks p 91
2. Kelly, G 1986. *Chief Executive Officers Success and the Development of High Potential Employees.* Johannesburg Unpublished M.B.A. Research Report: University of the Witwatersrand.
3. Ibid
4. Pruett, Q D 1989. Some Guidelines for Successful Management Development in South Africa. *South African Handbook of Managerial Development* vol 2, no 4, p 50–57.

Chapter I
1. Cooper, C and Arbrose, J 1984. Executive Stress Goes Global: *International Management* vol 39: p 28–32.
2. Kelly, G 1986. *Chief Executive Officers Success and the Development of High Potential Employees.* Johannesburg, unpublished M.B.A. Research Report: University of the Witwatersrand.
3. Peters, P J and Waterman, R H 1982. *In Search of Excellence.* New York: Harper and Row
4. Livingston, J S 1971. *Myth of the Well-Educated Manager.* Harvard Business Review. January — February: p 79–90.
5. Kotter, J P 1988. *The Leadership Factor.* New York: Free Press.
6. Senge, P 1990. *The Leaders New Work: Building Learning Organisations.* Sloan Management Review: Fall.
7. Hofmeyr, K 1989. *Why Employee Advancement Programmes Fail.* Institute of Personnel Management August 18–22.

137

8. Hall, J 1990. *A Premise of Competence.* Human Resource Management, February 14–17.
9. Bennis, W G 1988. *On Becoming a Leader.* Hutchinson Business Books, London.
10. Bennis, W G. Ibid.
11. *Fortune Magazine,* 1991. November U.S.A.
12. Charlton, G 1991. *Identifying Leadership Competence.* Johannesburg. Unpublished Masters of Management Thesis. University of the Witwatersrand.
13. Kouzes, J M *and* Posner, B Z 1988. *The Leadership Challenge: How to Get Extraordinary Things Done in Organisations.* San Francisco: Josey Bass.
14. Bennis, W G *and* Nanus, B 1985. *Leaders: The Strategies for Taking Charge.* New York: Harper and Row.
15. Kouzes, J M *and* Posner, B Z. Ibid.
16. Tucker, B 1991. *The Southern African Scenario — Key Challenges for Leadership.* Paper presented at the Leadership and Learning Conference, C.S.I.R. Pretoria, 12 May.
17. De Geus, A 1991. *Towards a National Extrovert Learning Culture.* Paper presented at the Leadership and Learning Conference, C.S.I.R. Pretoria, 12 May.
18. Senge, P. Ibid.
19. Carkhuff, R 1988. *Empowering the Creative Leader in the New Age of Capitalism.* Massachussets: Human Resource Press.
20. Boyatsis, R E 1982. *The competent Manager.* New York: Wiley p 12.
21. Drucker, P F 1074. *Management — Tasks, Responsibilities, Practices* (2nd Edition). London: Heinemann.
22. Carkhuff, R. Ibid.

Chapter II
1. Binidell, N 1990. Contents of a Strategic Human Resource Lecture — Wits Business School.
2. Naisbet, J *and* Aburdene, P 1990. *Megatrends 2000.*

3. Senge, P *The Fifth Discipline — The Art and Practice of Learning Organisations*. New York: Double Day Currency.

4. Deming, E 1991. *Leadership and Learning Brochure* — describing the Peter Senge book, The Fifth Discipline — Leadership and Learning Conference, C.S.I.R. Pretoria, 12 May.

5. Chinese Proverb — Kouzes, J M *and* Posner, B Z 1988. *The Leadership Challenge: How to get Extraordinary Things done in Organisations*. San Francisco: Josey Bass.

6. De Lange, J 1981. Report of the work committee, M.S.R.C. Investigation into Education. Pretoria. *Human Sciences research*, July.

7. Hofmeyr, K 1989. *Why Employee Advancement Programmes Fail. Institute of Personnel Management. August p 1822.*

8. Human, L 1989. *Management Development in a Changing Society*. Institute of Personnel Management. August p 8–11.

9. Hall, J 1990. A Premise of Competence. *Human Resource Management*. February p 14–17.

10. McClelland, D C 1973. Testing for Competence rather than Intelligence. *American Psychologist*. vol 28, no 7, p 1–14.

11. Bennis, W G 1984. The Four Competencies of Leadership. *Training and Development Journal*. August: p 15–19.

12. Kouzes, J M *and* Posner, B Z 1988. *The Leadership Challenge: How to get Extraordinary Thinge Done In Organisations*. San Francisco: Josey Bass.

13. Kouzes, J M and Posner, B Z. Ibid.

Chapter III

1. Zaleznik, A 1977. Managers and Leaders: Are They Different? *Harvard Business Review* Vol 55, No 5.

2. Zaleznik, A. Ibid.

3. Senge, P 1991. *The Fifth Discipline — The Art and Practice of Learning Organisations.* New York: Doubleday Currency.

4. Bennis, W G and Nanus, B 1985. *Leaders: Strategies For Taking Charge.* New York: Harpper and Row.

5. Zaleznik, A. Ibid.

6. McClelland, D C 1975. *Power: The Inner-Experience.* New York: Irvington Publishers.

7. Bennis, W G and Nanus, B. Ibid.

8. Senge, P. Ibid.

9. Frankl, V 1984. *Mans Search for Meaning.* Washington: Washington Squares Press.

10. Zaleznik, A. Ibid.

11. Human, L 1989. Management Development in a Changing Society. *Institute of Personnel Management.* August p. 8–11.

12. Senge, P. Ibid.

13. Manning, A D 1988. *The New Age Strategies.* Johannesburg: Southern Book Publishers.

14. Bennis, W G and Nanus, B. Ibid.

Chapter IV

1. Hersey, P and Blanchard, K 1982. *Management of Organisational Behaviour: Utilising Human Resources* 4th Edition. Englewood Cliff: Prentice Hall Inc.

2. Allport, F H 1924. *Social Psychology.* Boston.

3. Schein, E H 1980. *Organisational Culture and Leadership.* San Francisco: Josey Bass.

4. Bennis, W G and Nanus,B 1985. *Leaders: Strategies for Taking Charge.* New York: Harper and Row.

5. Lickert, R 1960. *A New Pattern of Management.* New York: McGraw Hill.

6. Limmerick, D C et al 1984. *Frontiers of Excellence: A Study of Strategy, Structure and Culture in 50 Australian Organisations. The Australian Institute of Management.*

7. Friedler, F E 1967. The Leadership Game: Matching the Man to the Situation. *Organisational Dynamics*. Winter p 11–12.

8. Kelly, G 1986. *Chief Executive Officers Success and the Development of High Potential Employees*. Johannesburg. Unpublished M.B.A. research report — Wits Business School.

9. Hersey, P *and* Blanchard. Ibid.

10. Schein, E H. Ibid.

11. Argyris, C. Leadership, Learning and Changing the Status Quo. *Organisational Dynamics*. Winter p 29–43.

12. Bennis, W G *and* Nanus, B. Ibid.

13. Frankl, V 1984. *Mans Search for Meaning*. Washington: Washington Squares Press.

14. Kouzes, J M *and* Posner, B Z. *The Leadership Challenge: How to get Extraordinary Things done in Organisations*. San Francisco: Josey Bass.

15. Senge, P 1991. *The Fifth Discipline* — The Art and Practice of Learning Organisations. New York: Double Day Currency.

16. Bennis, W G *and* Nanus, B. Ibid.

17. Kelly, G. Ibid.

18. Charlton, G 1991. *Identifying Leadership Competence*. Johannesburg. Unpublished Masters Thesis — Wits Business School.

19. Peters, T 1988. *The Leadership Alliance* — A Viewers Guide. California: Video Publishing House.

20. Human, L 1989. Management Development in a Changing Society. *Institute of Personnel Management*. August p 8–11.

21. Conger, J *and* Kanungo, R 1988. The Empowerment Process: Integrating Theory and Practice. *Academy of Management Review*, vol 13, no 3: p 471–482.

22. Carkhuff, R 1988. *Empowering the Creative Leader in the New Age of Capitalism.* Massachussets: Human Resource Press.

23. Boyatsis, R 1982. *The Competent Manager.* New York: Wiley.

24. McClagen, P 1983. *Models for Excellence* — Training and Development Competency Study Report. USA.

25. Boyatsis, R. Ibid.

26. McClelland, D C 1975. *Power: The Inner Experience.* New York: Irvington Publishers.

27. Sacht *et al* 1990. *Training and Development Report* (SA). Institute of Personnel Management.

28. McClagen, Ibid.

29. Fombrum, C; Tichey, N *and* Devanna, M 1984. *Strategic Human Resource Management.* New York: Wiley.

30. Kelly, G 1986. Ibid.

31. Bennis, W G *and* Nanus, B. Ibid.

32. Runyon, R P *and* Haber, A 1980. *Fundamentals of Behavioural Statistics.* Massuchussets: Adison Wesley.

Chapter V

1. Frankl, V 1984. *Mans Search for Meaning.* Washington: Washington Squares Press.

2. Frankl, Ibid.

3. Barker, J 1991. *The Power of Visions* — Videotape G.T.V. Video Distributors, Sandton.

4. *Developing a Philosophy of Management* 1991. U.C.T. Graduate School of Business. Face to Face Interviews (Videotape) involving top South African business leaders.

5. Ian McCraes *Vision for Escom* — Wits Business School lecture — 1991.

6. Senge, P 1991. *The Fifth Dicipline — The Art and Practice of Learning Organisations.* New York: Doubleday.

7. U.C.T. Business School, Ibid.

8. U.C.T. Business School, Ibid.

9. Luther King, M 1989. *The Words of Martin Luther King.* Fount Paperbacks: London.

10. Luther King, M in Senge, P 1990. *Vision, Leadership and Systems Thinking.* Papers presented at a seminar — Vaal Holiday Inn, Vanderbijlpark, June.

11. Campolo, A. *Tomorrow is Sunday* — Videotape — Million Dollar Round Table Conference, U.S.A.

Chapter VI

1. Bennis, W G 1984. The Four Competencies of Leadership. *Training and Development Journal.* August p 15–19.

2. Neal Chapman (Southern Life) — *Philosophy of Management Video* — U.C.T. Graduate School of Business Administration.

3. Ian McCrae (Escom). Ibid.

4. John Hall (Barlow Rand). Ibid.

5. Schein, E 1980. *Organisational Culture and Leadership.* San Francisco: Josey Bass.

6. Bobby Godsell (Anglo American) 1991. *Philosophy of Management.* Ibid.

7. Moss-Kanter, R 1989. The New Managerial Work, *Harvard Business Review*, November.

8. Kelly, G. 1986. *Chief Executive Officers Success and the Development of High Potential Employees.* Johannesburg. Unpublished M.B.A. research report — Wits Business School.

9. Hertzburg, F 1966. *Work and the Nature of Man.* Cleveland: World Publishing Company.

10. Frankl, V 1984. *Mans Search for Meaning.* Washington: Washington Squares Press.

11. Kouzes, J M and Posner, B Z 1988. *The Leadership Challenge: How to get Extraordinary Things done in Organisations.* San Francisco: Josey Bass.

12. Carkhuff, R 1988. *Empowering the Creative Leader in the New Age of Capitalism*. Massachussets: Human Resource Press.

13. Frankl, V 1977. *The Unconscious God*. London: Hudder and Stengton.

14. Kelly, G 1986. Ibid.

15. John Hall (Barlow Rand). *Developing a Philosophy of Management*. Ibid.

Chapter VII

1. Peter Searle (Volkswagen) 1991. *Developing a Philosophy of Management*. U.C.T. Business School Videotape.

2. Vic Hammond (Edgars) Ibid.

3. Ian McCrae (Escom) Ibid.

4. Kelly, G 1986. *Chief Executive Officers Success and the Development of High Potential Employees*. Johannesburg. Unpublished M.B.A. research report, Wits Business School.

5. Grant Thoman (Malbak) 1991. *Developing a Philosophy of Management*. Ibid.

6. Kouzes, J M and Posner, B Z 1988. *The Leadership Challenge: How to get Extraordinary Things done in Organisations*. San Francisco: Josey Bass.

7. Bennis, W G and Nanus, B 1985. *Leaders: Strategies for Taking Charge*. New York: Harper and Row.

8. Luther King, M 1989. *The Words of Martin Luther King*. Fount Paperbacks: London.

9. Carkhuff, R 1988. *Empowering the Creative Leader in the New Age of Capitalism*. Massachussets: Human Resource Press.

10. Kelly, G. Ibid.

11. Limmerick, D C 1990. Managers of Meaning: From Bob Geldofs Band-Aid to Australian C.E.O.'s *Organisational Dynamics* 22–23.

12. Charlton, G D 1991. *Identifying Leadership Competence.* Johannesburg. Unpublished M.A. Thesis — Masters in Human Resource Management — Wits Business School.

Chapter VIII

1. John Hall (Barlow Rand) 1991. *Developing a Philosophy of Management* Videotape — U.C.T. Graduate School of Business.
2. Neal Chapman (Southern Life). Ibid.
3. Mintzberg, H 1973. *The Nature of Managerial Work.* New York: Harper and Row.
4. Vaughn Beals — C.E.O. Harley Davidson — *The Leadership Alliance part II,* videotape produced by Tom Peters, Viewcom.
5. Taoist Story from Ancient China — cited in *Kouzes, J M and Posner, B Z 1988.*
6. Bennis, W G *and* Nanus, B 1985. *Leaders: Strategies for Taking Charge.* New York: Harper and Row.
7. Kelly, G 1986. *Chief Executive Officers Success and the Development of High Potential Employees.* Johannesburg: University of the Witwatersrand (unpublished M.B.A. research report).
8. Senge, P 1991. *The Fifth Discipline — The Art and Practice of Learning Organisations.* New York: Double Day Currency.
9. Boyatsis, R 1982, *The Competent Manager* New York: Wiley.
10. Limmerick, D C 1990. Managers of Meaning: From Bob Geldof's Band-Aid to Australian C.E.O.'s *Organisational Dynamics,* 22–23.
11. Senge, P 1991. Ibid.
12. Peters, T 1989. Leaders and Excellence in the 1990's: *South African Handbook of Management Development,* vol 2, no 11, p 5–9.
13. Kelly, G 1986. Ibid.

14. Ball, A *and* Asbury, S 1989. *The Winning Way.* Johannes-
    burg: Johnathon Ball Publishers.
15. Kouzes, J M *and* Posner, B Z 1988. *The Leadership Challenge:
    How to get Extraordinary Things done in Organisations.* San
    Francisco: Josey Bass.
16. Manning, A D 1988. *The New Age Strategies.* Johannes-
    burg: Southern Book Publishers.
17. Carkhuff, R 1988. *Empowering the Creative Leader in the
    New Age of Capitalism.* Massachusettes: Human Resource
    Press.

Chapter IX
1.   Hall, J 1990. A Premise of Competence. *Human Resource
     Management.* February p 14–17.
2.   Kouzes, T M *and Posner, B Z 1988. The Leadership Challenge:
     How to get Extraordinary Things done in Organisations.* San
     Francisco: Josey Bass.
3.   Eugene van As (Sappi). *Developing a Philosophy of Manage-
     ment.* U.C.T. Graduate School of Business — Videotape.
4.   Bennis, W G *and* Nanus, B 1985. *Leaders: Strategies for
     Taking Charge.* New York: Harper and Row.
5.   Peters, T 1989. Leaders and Excellence in the 1990's: *South
     African Handbook of Management Development* vol 2, no 11,
     p 5–9.
6.   Human, L 1989. Management Development in a Chang-
     ing Society. *Institute of Personnel Management.* August p
     8–11.
7.   Bobby Godsell (Anglo American) *Developing a Philosophy
     of Management.* Ibid.
8.   Jeff Liebesman (F.S.I.) Ibid.
9.   Vic Hammond (Edgars) Ibid.
10. Lapinsky, A 1990. *A Performance Based Approach to Man-
     agerial Competence.* University of the Witwatersrand (un-
     published M.M. thesis).

11. De Pree, M 1989. *Leadership Is An Art*. New York: Double-day.
12. Chamber of Mines 1991. *Strategic Career Progression Programme*.
13. Singer, B. The Future Focused Role Image — cited in Barker, J 1991. *The Power of Visions* — Videotape. G.T.V. Video Distributors, Sandton.
14. Blanchard, K 1991. *Leadership and the One Minute Manager*. Videotape, Mast Video Training, Johannesburg.

Chapter X
1. Kouzes, J M *and* Posner, B Z 1988. *The Leadership Challenge: How to get Extraordinary Things done in Organisations*. San Francisco: Josey Bass.
2. Hersey, P *and* Blanchard, K 1982. *Management of Organisational Behaviour: Utilising Human Resources. Prentice Hall International*.
3. Charlton, G 1991. *Identifying Leadership Competence*. Unpublished M.A. in management thesis — Wits Business School, Johannesburg.
4. Wade, C 1987. *Psychology*. New York: Wiley and Sons.
5. Baron, R A 1987. *Social Psychology: Understanding Human Interaction*. Boston: Harper and Row.
6. Bennis, W G *and* Nanus, B. *Leaders: Strategies for Taking Charge*. New York: Harper and Row.
7. McCormack, M 1991. *R.E.S. International Marketting Brochure*. Johannesburg.
8. Boyatsis, R 1982. *The Competent Manager*. New York: Wiley.
9. Luft, J 1970. *Group Processes: An Introduction to Group Dynamics*, 2nd edition. California: National Press Book.
10. Hersey, P *and* Blanchard, K 1982. Ibid.
11. Bennis, W 1989. *On Becoming a Leader*. Hutchinson Books: London.
12. Hersey, P *and* Blanchard, K 1982. Ibid.

13. Kelly, G 1986. *Chief Executive Officers Success and the Development of High Potential Employees.* (Unpublished M.B.A. research report — Wits Business School).
14. Boyatsis, R 1982. Ibid.
15. Bennis, W 1989. Ibid.
16. Kelly, G 1986. Ibid.
17. Bennis, W 1989. Ibid.
18. *Sunday Star Business Supplement* — 12 January, 1992.

Chapter XI
1. Bosman, H C 1991. *Mafeking Road.* Human and Rousseau: Johannesburg.
2. Kelly, G 1986. *Chief Executive Officers Success and the Development of High Potential Employees.* Unpublished M.B.A. research report — University of the Witwatersrand.
3. Hersey, P *and* Blanchard, K 1982. *Management of Organisational Behaviour: Utilising Human Resources.* Prentice Hall International.
4. Pruett, Q D 1989. Some Guidelines for Successful Management Development in *South Africa. South African Handbook of Management Development.*
5. Chamber of Mines Strategic Plan, 1990.
6. Chamber of Mines Strategic Plan, 1991.
7. Kelly, G 1986. Ibid.
8. Project Free Enterprise 1989. *Wealth Creation in South Africa.* School of Business Leadership, University of South Africa.
9. Cooper, C *and* Arbrose, J 1984. Executive Stress Goes Global: *International Management,* vol 39 p 28–32.
10. Project Free Enterprise, 1989. Ibid.